D1430069

Stars and Stripes for Éireann

Stars and Stripes for Éireann

American Connections in the making of Modern Ireland

Dermot Walsh

Published 2010
Oaneve Publishing, Limerick

ISBN
978-0-9565513-0-6

© Dermot Walsh 2010

All rights reserved. No part of this publication may be reproduced,
or transmitted in any form or by any means, including recording
and photocopying, without the written permission of the copyright holder,
application for which should be addressed to the publisher.
Written permission should also be obtained before any part of the
publication is stored in a retrieval system of any nature.

Disclaimer
Whilst every effort has been made to ensure that the contents
of this book are accurate, neither the publisher nor author can
accept responsibility for any errors or omissions or loss occasioned
to any person acting or refraining from acting
as result of any material in this publication.

Typeset by
Compuscript Ltd,
Bay 11a, Shannon Industrial Estate
Shannon, Co Clare.

Cover design by
Techgraph Graphic Design, Limerick

Printed by
Brunswick Press Ltd

This book is dedicated to the memory of the late Vincent Tobin
Captivating Bard and Weaver of Wonder Tales of Shannon

Contents

Stars from the Skies — Picture Profile Gallery

Acknowledgements

In recording the stories in this book, incalculable co-operation and practical assistance was willingly provided from an array of sources in the United States, also from Australia and in Ireland.

By preserving and knowing where to track down the script of a lecture on the restoration of Knappogue Castle delivered by the late Lavone Andrews, invaluable insights and details were provided from Mark Andrews III and Roseann Sessa, Vice President in charge of Marketing and Public Relations at his Castle Brands corporation in New York.

The facts of how syndicated travel columnist, Stanton Delaplane happened on and happened for Shannon Airport and Irish Coffee were opened up by his daughter, Kristin Delaplane Conti in San Francisco with background details filled in by the cuttings library and public information service at The San Francisco Chronicle.

Sincere thanks are due to Barbara de Lacy Hartigan for permission to use an extract from her book recalling her summer employment at Dromoland Castle Hotel and encounters with the mercurial owner, Bernard P. McDonough.

For guidance on the introduction to travellers to Irish Coffee at the Foynes flying boat base and the epic achievements of Charlie Blair and fellow flyers that placed Ireland on the transatlantic air charts and in an undisputed place of honour in the annals of commercial flight, I am indebted to Margaret O'Shaughnessy, heartbeat of the Foynes Flying Boat Museum and to Joe Lucey in Queensland, Australia for his remarkable powers of recall.

At the roots of what prompted this book and making the American connections documented here is the Brendan O'Regan Archive recorded for posterity in the years before the death of the late Dr. O'Regan in January 2008. For filling in accurate background details and guiding the chronological sequence of the stories related here, what could have amounted to deterring frustrations on research and checking were skirted by consulting "Bernard McDonough –

The Man and His Work" by Eugene C. Murdock (Marietta College Press, Ohio, 1988); "Red Ball In the Sky" by Charles F Blair (Jarrolds Publishing, 1970) and "The Billionaire Who Wasn't" by Conor O'Clery (Public Affairs, New York, 2007).

Without the limitless patience, unfailing perseverance and expert professional guidance of Morgan Lyons and Eimer Neville at Michael Cushley's **Compuscript** at Shannon Free Zone this book would never have reached publication stage. Similar qualities were demanded from Tony O'Loughlin of Techgraph Graphic Design, Limerick in coping with the whims and constant changes required by the author and fortunately his better judgement and visualisation gifts prevailed in the design for the cover. Undying gratitude is due for their contributions.

The gallery of pictures of movie stars from the vintage era of the cinema industry is included courtesy of the Vincent Tobin Archive.

Worthy of imperishable thanks is Aidan Corr who generously gave of his time and his dual expertise as fastidious printer and gifted writer for proof reading and correcting the text and bringing some semblance of order to the journalism.

Introduction

At what was to prove a most poignant "Farewell" that was seen and heard via the broadcast media of the world, President John F Kennedy gave his unintentional but nonetheless immeasurable imprimatur to Shannon Airport on the final Irish homecoming leg of his European tour of 1963.

"Ireland is an unusual place" the 35th President of the United States said "What happened 500 or 1,000 years ago is as yesterday. Where we are on the other side of the Atlantic, 3,000 miles away, we are next door". On the eve of his "goodbye", he had been seated beside "one of the most extraordinary women" in the person of the wife of the President of Ireland. President Kennedy told his airport audience that when he informed Sinead Bean de Valera that he was coming to Shannon, she had quoted lines of poetry that he had copied out.

The extract was from "'Tis" by the Limerick poet, novelist and playwright, Gerald Griffin and ran:

"'Tis the Shannon's brightly glancing
stream, brightly gleaming

Silent in the morning oh! the sight
entrancing
Thus return from travels long, years of
exile, years of pain
To see old Shannon's face again, o'er the
waters glancing.

The poem was in tribute to the river Shannon which in 20th century Ireland was bringing a great flow and tide of change to a country that was still in its formative stages in 1963. From the Shannon came the harnessed power of the river in which a fledgling Irish nation implemented one of the biggest engineering projects in Europe with the hydro electric scheme at Ardnacrusha that would bring the country from twilight to a new dawn of hope. Initiatives on opposite banks of the Shannon, first the Foynes flying boat base and later the land plane airport at Rineanna which would become Shannon, opened the imagination and welcoming hospitality embrace of Ireland to new thinking of new people from the New World, carried on the wings of the new phenomenon of civil aviation.

Through Shannon Airport gusted great winds of change that were transforming the fortunes not only of the county and region around the air terminal but would reach deep into the entire Irish economy and play a pivotal role in its development and planning. At Shannon Airport the unbounded imagination and flair of an extraordinary organisation, the Shannon Sales and Catering Service led by an extraordinary human being, Brendan O'Regan, attracted extraordinary allies. This book records some of those extraordinary events.

Dermot Walsh, 2010

Stan Delaplane: *He really made Irish Coffee*

The invention of Irish Coffee is claimed by the pioneering flying boat base of Foynes on the Limerick county banks of the river Shannon which has since themed a summer festival around the brew. It now transpires that while Irish Coffee got its international launch at Foynes, its originator knew the secret of the potion for some time before. But irrespective of the claims and the legends, it is an uncontestable fact that only for Stan Delaplane Irish Coffee would either have been forgotten or stayed as an Irish way of making the drinking of whiskey respectable by dressing it up in an alluring way.

It was a momentous start of a remarkable association when Stanton Delaplane made an unscheduled stop at Shannon Airport in the winter of 1950. Like all seasoned newspapermen of that era a stopover on any journey was reason enough to search out a bar and a drink. But this time he really needed a drink because his plane had lost an engine on the stretch of sky across the Atlantic from Newfoundland. That was the reason why the plane had headed for Shannon as the nearest airport. And like all good newspapermen, Stanton Delaplane was always on the lookout for a good story. At the Shannon Airport bar he got both.

It was not quite divine intervention that brought Stanton Delaplane to Ireland but there was a touch of religion involved. It was 1950 and a Holy Year in which Roman Catholics all over the world made a special effort to make a pilgrimage to the Vatican seat of the church's supreme pontiff. Delaplane was on a press trip to Rome as one of an elite group of newspaper columnists including his New York contemporary of legend, Earl Wilson and Bob Considine who was a syndicated columnist with the Randolph Hearst chain of newspapers.

As Delaplane recalled in a radio interview years later, his anxiety about flying and any grain of religion within him were brought together on that Atlantic crossing. "We had a bunch of priests on the flight with us and we seemed to stop everywhere for gas. I had a priest sitting next to me and every time we'd take off he would cross himself. Then we lose an engine. The priest was now crossing himself as we flew and he's also doing a few laps around the beads too".

They made it to Shannon where they stayed for a couple of days while their plane got an engine refit. Like countless other passengers who were held up by weather conditions or technical troubles, they stayed at "The Camp", a cluster of chalets on the fringe of the airport laid on for just such contingencies as well as providing accommodation for airport workers.

During the Shannon stop over, the man from the San Francisco Chronicle was introduced to Irish Coffee at the bar in the airport transit area where the first Duty Free Store in the world was just starting to take shape. In giving Irish Coffee a try Delaplane was to give Shannon Airport and Irish tourism, Irish whiskey exports and a bar-restaurant in his home city a gigantic shot in the arm.

While the good looking concoction went down just right with Delaplane, the bonus for the newspaper man was that there was also a good story to it. And there was no shortage of people around Shannon Airport to tell and to embroider the story.

The story began with a chef named Joe Sheridan and the sense of style and confidence that the air age brought to an impoverished west of Ireland. The opportunity for an obscure and struggling new nation to take its place on the world map was recognised and grasped by the government when taking the chance ahead of its UK neighbours to provide the first stop in Europe for unproven trans-Atlantic flight. Flying boat services began into Foynes from 1937 and in 1942 Ireland put its imprint on the war-time connection between the USA and Britain when taking over the catering service at the flying boat base.

The young man who was hand-picked by top ranking government ministers and officials was Brendan O'Regan and from the start he resolved to bring a sense of style and sophistication to the operation where the elite classes flying the Atlantic got their first impressions and taste of Ireland. The art and antiquities expert John Hunt was brought in to oversee the interior decoration at the Foynes restaurant where O'Regan insisted that the young women serving the customers had to be educated and confident in looking after what were essentially all-VIP passenger lists. Regardless of the warmth of the Foynes reception and hospitality however, even the record crossings of the Atlantic of 15 hours and more duration meant that passengers arrived at Foynes cramped and chilled. It was to revive tired bodies and spirits that Foynes regularly provided a greeting of coffee laced with Irish whiskey. But Brendan O'Regan wanted something more sophisticated and asked chef Joe Sheridan to brew up something "with eye appeal". Soon afterwards the chef presented O'Regan with the distinctive Irish Coffee which became a staple at Foynes and later at Shannon Airport when land planes brought the romance of the flying boats to a close.

Joe Lucey, who was getting the best possible grounding as O'Regan's Number 2 at the outset of a career that took him to the top in hotel management, could recall how Irish Coffee enhanced the Irish welcome at Foynes. More than 60 years on and living in Australia, he remembered –"sometimes when the sea-planes could not take off and delayed by inclement weather for several hours, passengers and crew were transferred to the restaurant where they had their meal a couple of hours earlier. On such occasions, chef Sheridan, after consulting Brendan O'Regan and the airline management, recommended serving his own style coffee. After these first tastings, his Irish Coffee was received with applause by the passengers and management. After a month or two the popularity of this new drink was to spread to a few of the Limerick city hotels and to the bar at the land planes base at Rineanna".

But Joe Lucey could also set the record straight about where Irish Coffee actually originated. Then working in the bar and lounge he shared a room at Foynes with Chef Sheridan in 1943 and as room-mates they talked about their family backgrounds. The chef had brought the secret of Irish Coffee with him to Foynes and had recalled it from his youth when Brendan O'Regan looked for something special for his passengers. He confided to Joe Lucey that as a boy he had accompanied his father to cattle markets around north county Dublin and to counteract the chill of early winter mornings, his father and fellow cattle dealers would lace their coffee with whiskey. It was in those youthful years that the aspiring chef experimented with coffee, whiskey and cream when tumbling to the chemistry formula that the cream would float on the coffee surface only when supported by a generous helping of sugar in advance.

Whatever its origins, Irish Coffee made its international debut at Foynes and had become the speciality of the house at the Shannon Airport bar when Stan Delaplane was building on the talent that had made him only the third California journalist to win a Pulitzer Prize and also building the readership that would put his words on the breakfast tables of three million readers six days a week as a syndicated columnist.

The journalist carried back such pleasant memories of Irish Coffee that he regularly gave it a mention in his column, so much so that two years on he was pressed into trying his own hand at making it himself.

He had called into one of his regular haunts the Buena Vista on Fisherman's Wharf and the events of that night became part of San Francisco drinking lore. It was November 10th, 1952 and there were few witnesses to what happened. As Delaplane recalled, "the Buena Vista was kind of dying at the time and there were only three guys on the stools. There was me, Tom Rooney who ran the Sports and Boat Show and down at the end of the bar a real drunk of a reporter that we had who would drink anything as long as it had liquor in it".

With not a great deal to occupy them, the owner of the "Buena Vista", Jack Koeppler put it to Delaplane –"what's that Irish Coffee you've been writing about that you were served at Shannon Airport?" To which Delaplane replied –"Give me some Irish whiskey and I'll show you". So began a series of initially vain attempts to follow the recipe format that had been entrusted to Delaplane at Shannon. But various combinations and permutations of the formula fell flat. Or more exactly the cream went flat. Their frustration was balanced up by the happy gratitude of the reporter at the end of the bar who became the disposal unit for the rejected efforts.

"I don't know what the hell is the matter," Delaplane told Jack Koeppler. "I know that it floats in Ireland". And Delaplane recollected in later years –"So we figured out that the cream in Ireland is heavier. Of course, the more sugar you put in it, the more lift it has. It rides on top better if you've got a thicker substance below. So Jack put the cream in the mixer for a couple of seconds, just enough to float it, which is the way they do it now. It wasn't really whipped cream but at least it would stay up". The then mayor of San Francisco would lend a helping hand later. Mayor George Christopher was also the owner of a large dairy. He put his chemists to work and the solution they came up with was to "age" the cream for 48 hours and then froth it to the consistency of pancake batter. Their trials and tests also let them in on one element of Joe Sheridan's secret –heating the stemmed glass was the essential first step.

Two years after Delaplane had tasted Irish Coffee for the first time at Shannon it became an overnight sensation in San Francisco. "People started coming into the Buena Vista and trying it". It would be years later that Delaplane would write about the Buena Vista, but the taste for Irish Coffee simply took off. While the bar had been in serious decline the night they cracked the correct way of making it, the bar became the "in" place. "Pretty soon you had cars outside, mink coats coming in after the theatre and things like that," Delaplane recalled.

The Buena Vista owner Jack Koeppler became a champion of the Irish Coffee drink and in Delaplane's words "regarded this as a holy war of some sort". With 20 Irish Coffees at a time being lined up on the bar counter to meet demand, Koeppler left the running of the Buena Vista to his partner George Freeberg and took off on missions to win over converts to Irish Coffee. "He went up to Reno and made Irish Coffee for gambling joints there," Delaplane recorded.

At the Buena Vista, an Irish Coffee Club was established with Delaplane as Founder and Chief Inspector and Chef Joe Sheridan installed as Chief Inspector in Ireland. Membership cards were issued to more than a hundred supporters.

Stan Delaplane's fondness for retelling the Irish Coffee story reached hugely expanded readership from 1952 when his five days a week "Postcard" travel column was running in up to 45 newspapers in the latter half of the 1950s. The appetite of his readers for the Irish Coffee story proved to be a match for the American taste for the drink. The columnist first wrote about Irish Coffee and Shannon after that 1950 visit. He returned the following year and recycled the story in his column once again. A year on he was back in Shannon as part of his European travels but decided to give the Irish Coffee story a rest. The columnist was surprised to receive a bunch of letters asking why he had not written about Irish Coffee this time round. "It was the only time I've ever had people ask why didn't you do it?" he recalled.

Down at the Buena Vista where sipping an Irish Coffee became a "must" along with a streetcar ride for any visitor to San Francisco the bar was the toast of the Irish distilling industry. Before

Irish Coffee, the bar ordered in 12 cases of Irish whiskey a year. Once Irish Coffee fever took hold, yearly consumption soon soared to 1,200 cases. Such was the impact on sales of Irish whiskey in the United States that the Irish Export Board sent an emissary to San Francisco in 1957 to credit Delaplane with the steep rise in Irish whiskey sales which in the first seven months of that year were equal to total 1955 sales. It was a major boost for Irish exports, as Irish whiskey sales of around thirty thousand dollars a year were straggling way behind Scotch with sales of 87million dollars. With such a massive gap, the Irish Export Board was only too willing to play up the story of how a newspaperman popularised Irish Coffee.

Eventually both ends of the Irish Coffee story would be brought together. That was when Chef Joe Sheridan, who had introduced Irish Coffee to Americans at Foynes in 1943, came to work in San Francisco. He had been lured away from Shannon Airport by Trans Canada Airlines which hired him as head chef for its Toronto Airport restaurant. He was to spend part of a nomadic career as chef at Tiny's Waffle Restaurant in the city where his Irish Coffee was immortalized and sold up to 2,000 glasses per day at the height of its popularity at the Buena Vista.

There were even spin-off benefits to the flagship Irish craft industry of Waterford Crystal. With Irish Coffee in vogue as a sophisticated manner of drinking whiskey, it was suggested to the revived hand-cut crystal firm that an Irish Coffee glass would be just right for the American market and an ideal gift purchase by visiting American tourists. The suggestion came from Joe Lucey, the old Foynes hand who had been in on the birth of Irish Coffee who had risen to general manager of the Great Southern Hotel chain operated by the State-run transport company. In what was then the leading hotel group in the country, he had gift shops in each hotel which were outlets and showcases for Waterford Crystal. Once he had convinced Con Dooley, the export manager at Waterford Crystal, he also contacted his mentor at Foynes Brendan O'Regan at his Sales and Catering Service at Shannon Airport. Between them, they put in an order for twelve thousand Irish Coffee glasses.

Irish Coffee and Stanton Delaplane were made for each other. The story behind Irish Coffee provided an instant hook on which a journalist could hang a story and the Irish roots of the story made it the ideal vehicle for blarney and spinning a good yarn.

The Delaplane touch that characterised the column that he wrote until the eve of his death at age 80 in 1988 is illustrated in the way that Delaplane could take something as commonplace as a recipe and turn it into a saga of romance and dark deeds.

When the man from the Irish Export Board came to San Francisco to honour Delaplane and Irish Coffee, he turned to the conventional step by step guide to the making of Irish Coffee which was reproduced on countless tea towels, mugs and other souvenirs from Ireland.

"A drink rich as an Irish brogue
Strong as a friendly hand
Sweet as the tongue of a rogue
And smooth as the wit of the land"

As told Delaplane-style, the recipe was the very same, but the telling was completely different. As documented in "The Little World of Stanton Delaplane", one of the two collections of his best columns which both made the New York Times best sellers list, the story went – " A chef by the name of Sheridan invented Gaelic Coffee said the man at the Shannon Airport. Surely said Joe Sheridan we must invent a stirrup cup for poor souls and them not able to put their shivering hands in their pockets for a shilling to pay unless we warm them. What is more warming, said Joe Sheridan, than Irish whiskey smooth as a maiden's kiss. To take the chill from their poor shaking hands we will fill the glass with coffee black as Cromwell's heart. We will top it off with a floating inch of Irish cream."

The way in which Stanton Delaplane told his stories was polished over a newspaper career in which he distinguished himself in all aspects of his craft. He was born in Chicago but his family moved to California and having got a taste for journalism on his college paper got a job on the Santa Barbara Morning News at age eighteen. He had clocked up experience at a couple of further titles in his local area before being turned down for a job at the San Francisco Chronicle when he was 21. At age 23 he was editing an up-market magazine and demonstrated his appreciation of quality writing and why he was in the job when he bought four short stories from William Saroyan a couple of years before he was acclaimed as a master of the genre. "He wanted to buy a car and needed the money," Delaplane would modestly recall.

He was back knocking on the door of the San Francisco Chronicle in 1936 and this time he was taken on to start a 52 year stint on the paper that was broken only by war-time service with the US Maritime Commission and even then his by-line was appearing as Chronicle war correspondent in the Pacific.

The gifts for distilling information into eye-catching snappy journalese which characterised the enduring appeal of Delaplane's columns were evident from his early days at the Chronicle. Initially he was re-working publicity handouts and then moved to "The World", the paper's weekly magazine. As recalled in later years by contemporaries, his prolific re-write skills were polishing up 24,000 words per week - an assignment which required the input of 5 journalists when he moved up six months later to editor of the women's page.

His writing talent and his eye for the offbeat made him an outstanding news reporter of his day and won recognition with the 1942 Pulitzer Prize for a series of articles on a movement by a cluster of counties in California and Oregon to break away and form what would at that time have been the 49th State. Four years later he was awarded the first of his National Headliners Club awards – this time for his feature writing.

The new post World War II world was smaller and the war-driven advances in air travel were bringing once faraway places within reach and Stanton Delaplane was in the front line as a travel writer. His pursuit of the odd and whimsical, the personalities and nuggets of unusual information that caught his fancy and which he shared with his readers meant that he spent up to five months of the year travelling. As in his first encounter with Irish Coffee, whenever he took to the North Atlantic air route to and from Europe in the 1950s, the re-fuelling stop at Shannon became a stop over for the travel writer too. When the advent of the jet and mass travel eliminated the re-fuelling stop at Shannon, he continued to visit Ireland and the west of Ireland in particular.

He was a household name in journalism and the travel trade and merited an entry in "Who's Who in America" by the 1960s. His profile was added to with a second National Headliners Club award in 1959 when the citation was for the best travel writing in any American newspaper and a silver plaque from the Pacific Area Travel Association in 1961 for the best travel series. Collections of his best columns had made the best sellers lists and he also wrote "Delaplane in Mexico" and "Pacific Pathways" in the opening half of the 1960s. In between he had also recorded life with his daughter Kristin ("Kris") in a feature series which prompted comparisons with James Thurber when published in book form under the title "And How She Grew".

Even at the height of his profession Stanton Delaplane was doing favours for Irish tourism and especially for Shannon Airport and what seemed a conveyor belt of innovations that were being dreamed to maintain and grow the flow of American visitors.

In his weekday "Stan Delaplane's Postcard" which lived up to its name with crisp but engaging travel information, the power of the column and the Delaplane name was demonstrated in less than 35 words. Memorised for decades thereafter by Shannon promoters was the succinct message – "Shannon, Ireland. Over at the village of Quin near Shannon Airport they are thinking of building thatched cottages for rental by the week or the month. For details write Brendan O'Regan, Shannon Airport, Ireland".

Seven hundred replies were received. For some time before Brendan O'Regan's Shannon Development had been brain-storming for ideas that would spread American tourists beyond the primary visitor centres and into the heartland and cultural core of the country. Bringing that about would also require a move away from the coach tours to Bunratty, Killarney and other points and into the fly-drive era of independent travel and self-catering.

The responses prompted by the Delaplane mention were used as a mailing list for a questionnaire to test out genuine interest from the American market and judge if the concept was viable.

The feedback from the USA was the clincher in the decision to move ahead with the establishment of Rent-an-Irish Cottage which bonded villages with the State promoters in a partnership arrangement which gave the locals not only a say but also a direct interest in making the cottage guests happy and the cottage scheme a success.

The village of Quin with its imposing medieval abbey remnants was the original setting that Brendan O'Regan had in mind for the first cluster of cottages but the unpredictable vagueries and twists of local opinion and debate dictated otherwise. But where to make a start became a matter of great contention.

The village of Ballyvaughan below Black Head on the Clare shores of Galway Bay was suggested. Deprived and denuded by absence of local opportunity and consequent emigration and migration, Ballyvaughan was a forlorn fishing hamlet with very little going for it and much the same to show for it. While there were very serious doubts and skeptics, it was decided to go for it at Ballyvaughan and to rectify the shabby state that the village had fallen into with a community-based scheme which gave a boost to local morale as well as the streetscape of the village.

The twin clusters of cottages at Ballyvaughan sparked a revival which gained in momentum for the area through the following four decades. From its 1969 start the Rent-an-Irish Cottage combination of rustic charm with modern day comforts including under-floor heating was brought to a dozen villages around Shannon. But even more important that its role in bringing tourism to previously bypassed areas, Rent-an-Irish Cottage set the standards for the waves of private investment in self-catering holiday developments and holiday homes which flowed through coastal areas and beauty spots throughout the country in subsequent decades.

Ballyvaughan and its cottages became synonymous with and a symbol of quality self-catering accommodation and generated year-round business with overseas visitors in the peak summer months and home demand propping up the rest of the year with Christmas a guaranteed sell-out. The activity stimulated by the cottages began a chain-reaction which attracted new investment in further holiday developments and holiday homes and in restaurants, craft shops and other facilities that transformed the run-down village of Ballyvaughan into the linchpin of a flagship centre of rural-based enterprise built on making others feel at home.

A plaque honouring Chef Joe Sheridan as the inventor of Irish coffee adorns the bar in the transit area location of the Duty Free Store at Shannon Airport. As the man who popularised Irish Coffee and who, unknowingly, turned the tide for Ballyvaughan and it counterpart villages, something similar is richly deserved by Stanton Delaplane.

Charlie Blair: *Air age legend connected flight eras*

Setting a new first was the furthest thing from the mind of the pilot as he and his crew made the last minute checks in the cockpit of the Sikorsky VS 44 flying boat "Excalibur". The preoccupying thoughts were for the passenger list of sixteen that included top military brass and diplomats whose movements were under tight war-time security and undeniably also under enemy surveillance.

Captain Charles F Blair had learned to fly before taking his degree in science and mechanical engineering at the University of Vermont and service with the Naval Reserve that included a stint at the Naval Flying School in Pensacola, Florida. At the start of a flying career that would set him apart as a master of the airways, he was part of the pioneering development of civil aviation in the United States during seven years with United Airlines when he was largely on mail runs across the rugged terrain of the western states of the USA.

In 1940 he was named chief pilot of the newly formed American Export Airlines which would subsequently evolve into American Overseas Airlines and later still be absorbed into the Pan American carrier. American Export Airlines was the new challenger to the flag carrier airlines British Overseas Airways and Pan Am which had carved up transatlantic air travel with the flying boat services that were charting new eras of transport and communications. With Charlie Blair in command of every route-mapping survey flight and each of the inaugural flights that opened up connections from the United States to South America, Africa and the British Isles, firsts were being added to the early chapters of aviation history almost every time he took off. His airline tapped into his reputation among airmen, his experience and his contacts when putting the chief pilot in charge of recruitment and training of pilots who had to master the balance of seamanship and flying expertise that was imperative for the testing long haul flights over stages of landings, uplift of fuel and provisions and take offs that often extended over twenty four hours.

Setting a pattern for his future life in the air, Charlie Blair was the test pilot during four months of proving trials for the new Sikorsky S-44 which were mostly flown in the longer daylight hours of Florida from mid January 1942. Never before had he taken a maiden flight with an aircraft straight off the drawing board, so by mid year nobody was more familiar with the capability and longer range edge over competition of the new flying boat than Captain Blair.

On March 2nd, 1942 Blair piloted "Excalibur" on its survey flight to the Foynes flying boat base that had brought Ireland into the world aviation picture. Four months later, when he was two weeks short of his thirty-third birthday, the big Sikorsky bird churned up the waters of the river Shannon before heading out on its first westward crossing of the Atlantic with passengers and mail.

It was to be no ordinary crossing but then it was no ordinary passenger list and at a time and place that were far from ordinary.

For a tiny pocket of Ireland, the coming of the flying boats and the outbreak of World War II had combined in what was akin to a H.G. Wells "Time Machine" effect which projected a small patch of county Limerick forward into what was virtually a time zone that was years if not decades ahead of the rest of the country. In an Ireland that was still struggling to break out of deep-rooted economic stagnation and social deprivation, a different world was alive and functioning almost in secret in a tightly-knit rural society.

Thanks to its natural assets of a sheltered port alongside a wide expanse of clear deep waters and flat land, the village of Foynes had been plucked from obscurity and rushed from easy paced living to high-speed urgency when it was picked out to be the flying boat base that would bring the continents of Europe and North America closer together. Already established as dominant forces in their field, British Overseas Airways Corporation and Pan American Airways were made welcome by an eagerly co-operative Irish government that recognised the opening up of transatlantic aviation as a way for the new Irish state to pin its economic aspirations to the tail of the age of the airplane.

The transatlantic negotiations between the governments of the United States, Great Britain and Ireland and those involving the airlines as well as the ground-breaking effort that went into setting up a flying boat base and its extensive services proved frustratingly ill-timed. The first flight by a Pan American Boeing 314 took off on June 28th, 1939 and just over two months later came the outbreak of World War II. The British Overseas Airways Corporation had taken on the management of the Foynes base and the catering facilities that were going to be an imperative need for transatlantic travellers who would spend most of 24 hours in the air between the two continents. But BOAC had to withdraw from Foynes because Britain was a combatant in the war declared on Germany and Ireland was neutral. However the Irish form of neutrality was probably at its most subtle and also hidden from all but the most knowing eyes in and around the Foynes flying boat base.

Wartime Foynes became one of the most cosmopolitan centres of movement on either side of the Atlantic and also a key staging point in wartime power and planning. Transiting through Foynes came top military brass travelling incognito in civilian dress, faces from the Cabinet room at London's Downing Street and the diplomatic circuit in Washington D.C. that would have been instantly recognised elsewhere, aristocrats and bluebloods from old European royal lines uprooted by the war and VIPs that included scientists and wives of wartime strategists and decision makers who traveled under a double cloak of tight security and anonymity. There were watchful eyes around Foynes and not all belonged to the men of G2, the Intelligence unit of the Irish Army.

It was as if a secret colony had been transplanted into the wedge of countryside between Foynes and the picture postcard village of Adare. Moving to and fro through the flying boat base were generals and admirals in mufti, statesmen and diplomats with their aides, scientists and government officials. They not only broke their journey at Foynes. Quite often the predatory Luftwaffe activity in the skies over the Atlantic and weather hazards could hold up flight departure for days and required the passengers to stop over at the Dunraven Arms Hotel which, like most of the visually enchanting Tudor-style streetscape of the village, owed its origins to the enlightened local development policies of the landlord Earls of Dunraven whose Adare Manor and estate was the pride and centrepiece of the village.

Upper class British tones were not out of place in the stately 18th century hotel and overseas accents and Yankee twangs were not uncommon or an object of curiosity to locals. Here, in a quiet corner of a quiet land where the upper classes traditionally made their playground, the high and the mighty were inconspicuous and low key. Any passenger boarding a flying boat at Foynes was either exceptionally well off financially or of exceptional importance in the war effort or in international relations. Back then the cost of a one way flight was $375 and a return flight $675(which equates to $2,250 and $4,050 in 2009 values) and was the standard rate at a time when $5,000 a year was a handsome upper class income.

That all was not what it seemed around the flying boat base was equally true in the air. It would be most of a decade before it emerged that the new American Export Airlines service was actually a creation of the military arm of the US government. In what would presage the under cover activities of the Central Intelligence Agency (CIA) in Vietnam of the 1960s and in later theatres of conflict, the civilian American Export Airlines was a flag of convenience that brought into use the long range Vought-Sikorsky VS-44 flying boat, only three of which were ever built and had originally been committed to fly for the US Navy.

In the depths of World War II, the Foynes base was the busiest flying boat junction in Europe and favoured by the transatlantic airlines because take up of fuel at the Foynes stopover meant extra onboard carrying capacity which was worth an estimated twelve hundred to fifteen hundred pounds Sterling in payload. American Export Airlines joined Pan American and British Overseas Airways on the Foynes run from mid-1942 and in the subsequent twelve months 1,500 flights were routed through the base and carried 15,000 passengers.

The exalted status and rank of the air travellers and the most opaque veils of secrecy surrounding their movements were exemplified in the passenger list on that flight out of Foynes on Sunday, June 22nd, 1942. On board the first westward flight with passengers and mail were four senior pilots on familiarisation training, a couple of ambassadors and Admiral Sir Andrew Cunningham, Commander of the Mediterranean Fleet who was on his way to Washington D.C. for top secret planning of the Allied invasion of North Africa. Aides and lower rank military personnel were among the total of sixteen passengers.

The flying boat "Excalibur" followed the sun, taking off late into the longest day of the year so that the Atlantic crossing would be largely under cover of darkness. Initially flying at 1,000 feet, as the night closed in Captain Blair brought the flight path up to 8,000 feet for a closer view of the constellations of the sky for age-old navigation guidance. But progress at the upper altitude was slowed by headwinds and the word coming in over the radio was not encouraging. The flight plan was for "Excalibur" to fly from Foynes to the edge of Newfoundland for uptake of fuel at Botwood, a flight of fourteen hours duration. But weather updates reported that drizzle and fog were covering the Bay of Exploits and Captain Blair decided to go for an alternative landing area.

The next option was Shediac in New Brunswick, Canada, but the weather bulletins indicated that what was usually an ideal staging post for flying boats was also enveloped in fog.

There was only one choice left. That was Halifax on Nova Scotia's east coast.

Now needing to squeeze the maximum distance out of his fuel tanks, Captain Blair took "Excalibur" out of the grip of the headwind that was resisting the flying boat and costing precious gasoline. He brought the flying boat down to an altitude of a couple of hundred feet above the Atlantic waves and reduced the revolutions of the four great engines powering the propellers.

Suddenly what had been a mounting state of tension and uncertainty as to whether fuel supplies would last until a safe haven was reached, "Excalibur" was purring along. Released from the battle against the headwind, the flying boat was doing a steady maritime speed of 110 knots. With the headwind's resistance removed, "Excalibur" was covering more ocean to the gallon and as the seaplane burned up fuel with every mile the load was being lightened and more distance per gallon was being achieved. Now there was no apprehension about reaching Halifax. Even when word came over the air that a Halifax stop also posed a hazard with low cloud and harbour swells, the performance of the big Sikorsky under Captain Blair's handling injected calm confidence. When miles to go were measured against the metred levels of what remained in the fuel tanks, the skipper floated the thought – "Suppose we give Halifax a miss? Maybe we can go all the way?"

Confident that his planning of test flights and trial runs had acquainted him with safe harbours in between where he could set down the flying boat if calculations proved faulty, Captain Blair headed for New York.

It was the afternoon of Monday, June 23rd when passengers on "Excalibur" clapped eyes on the Whitestone Bridge in New York Harbour. Coming into Flushing Bay, the pilot switched to the last tank of fuel. Just under a full load of 3,820 gallons had been uploaded from the floating tenders at Foynes the previous day. Now less than 100 gallons remained. Yet there were 95 gallons to spare when the flying boat moored.

The flight – the first direct westward commercial crossing from Foynes to New York carrying passengers and mail – had taken 25 hours and 40 minutes. Whatever the timing, it was a record making run. It was also a first. That the knighted seadog was very much aware of just what he and his fellow passengers had been party to was conveyed in his typically British low key but significance-laden remark as he disembarked. As Charlie Blair's autobiographical "Red Ball in the Sky" recorded, Admiral Sir Andrew Cunningham commented "remarkable voyage". Not flight, but voyage. A tacit salute from an eminent navy man to the seamanship as well as the flying expertise of the captain.

In the remaining years of World War II Charlie Blair would chalk up new records almost every time he took the seat behind the controls. In 1943 he proposed and then flew the first winter airline service on the North Atlantic run, flying non stop between the US and Britain. In many cases he was bettering his own records. In 1944 for example he was pilot in command for the five fastest seaplane crossings of the Atlantic – with new records set over five consecutive flights. By then, he had brought the duration of the flight down to 14 hours, 17 minutes.

But it was an all time record that placed him above all other aviators. A record that would remain unrivalled for all time. That record of all records was achieved on the route between Ireland and New York and was set in two differing flying modes. On October 22, 1945, Captain Charles F. Blair took the flying boat "Excalibur" out of Foynes for the last time. On that milestone day that marked the end of an era, hundreds turned out to witness the event. Captain Blair brought the great VS 44 into Flushing Bay on October 23rd and in the same day switched to a land plane out of La Guardia Airport and piloted the DC 4 into the new air terminal at Rineanna which would become Shannon Airport. Two overnights. Two crossings of the Atlantic. It would never happen again because it could never happen again.

Little wonder then that Charlie Blair was an idolised hero of the romantic pioneer days of transatlantic flight. He moved with the times in aviation and Ireland also moved with the times. The new air terminal for land planes at Rineanna was on the opposite bank of the river Shannon to the flying boat base at Foynes. In anticipation of a transition phase in the movement from flying boat to land planes, the selection of the Rineanna site had been influenced by the adjacent amenity of a lagoon where in the earliest development stage of the airport, a basin was shaped that could accommodate no less than fifteen flying boats. And another basin was actually planned but never materialised. The catering operation that had won Ireland international acclaim and set standards of excellence that would later guide the formation of a national tourism industry switched locations from Foynes to Rineanna. That change meant that Brendan O'Regan too made the change and, like Charlie Blair, was also building his legend.

In the archive recordings made before the end of his long and achievement-studded life, Brendan O'Regan would recall the celebrity status of the aviators that included Charlie Blair. When the transatlantic flights rolled up to the new Irish airport, the passengers did not disembark before the captain and crew. "Led by the captain and his uniformed crew, the passengers would march in parade down through the airport building. They would promenade down the corridor to the lounge which introduced the passengers to the restaurant on one side and the shop on the other," O'Regan would recollect. The restaurant, operating round the clock in the unpredictable comings and goings of transatlantic flights, won the airport and "Shannon training" international repute and the shop became the first airport Duty Free Store in the world.

Charlie Blair's career and achievements simply soared to new heights with each unfolding phase of civil aviation development. He commanded the early test and subsequent scheduled flights of Lockheed Constellations and Boeing statocrusisers on the North Atlantic and served with Pan American when American Export Airlines merged with the great rival from the flying boat days in 1950. Wherever he encountered caution, he did things his own way. In a privately owned and personally modified P 51 Mustang fighter he tagged onto high altitude westerly winds to fly from New York to London Heathrow at an average 446 miles an hour, setting a record of 7 hours, 48 minutes for a transatlantic crossing by piston engine plane that also remains unsurpassed. That was in January 1951 and four months later he piloted the same plane on the first solo flight over the Artic and North Pole by a single engine aircraft. That non stop flight of 10 hours and 27 minutes proved the accuracy of a system of navigation that had been developed by Charles F Blair.

His airmanship and proven technical skills were also in demand from the US military. He was commissioned a Colonel in the Air Force Reserve in April 1953 and flew most of the first time aircraft test runs for the US Air Force, including numerous supersonic flights. He was back making history on the Atlantic in 1956 when he led three F84F fighters on the first non-stop flight across the Atlantic, taking the Great Circle Route. Three years later he commanded the first non stop flight over the North Pole by jet fighters, leading two F-100s from Weathershield RAF station England to Eielson US Air Force base in Alaska.

Outside his military engagements as test pilot and consultant which brought him to the rank of Brigadier General in the Air Force Reserve, he was also in the air in his own private sector venture. He set up his own Associated Air Transport non-scheduled airline, flying its only C 46 aircraft on long haul runs between New York, Europe, the Middle East and South America. He completed sixteen million passenger miles before selling the operation.

In nineteen years as a senior pilot with Pan American Airways from its 1950 takeover of American Overseas Airways, Charlie Blair was a fixture on long haul routes to Europe and South America. His years of service marked the changeover from propeller driven to jet aircraft and predictably he was one of the first to pilot a Pan Am jet liner.

Five years before his 1969 retirement from Pan Am at age 60, he returned to his great love, the flying boat, when he founded Antilles Air Boats in the Virgin Islands. Love of a different kind was to crown a life of a hero figure in a world of glamour and excitement when he married a movie queen. In 1968 he married Maureen O'Hara who, as the teenage Maureen FitzSimons, had rocketed to instant stardom in Alfred Hitchcock's "Jamaica Inn" and teamed up again with screen giant Charles Laughton when they went to Hollywood to co-star in "The Hunchback of Notre Dame". It was the third marriage for both of them and for Maureen O'Hara the partnership "with the love of my life".

On his retirement from Pan America the couple moved to an idyllic life on the Virgin Islands where Captain Blair piloted his Antilles Air Boats venture to new heights, building up to a fleet of 23 amphibious aircraft which operated 120 flights a day and carried 150,000 passengers a year on Caribbean runs. Still flying 40-50 hours per week, he was at the controls of one of the airline's 19 Grumman Goose flying boats when it crashed and he was killed instantly on September 2, 1978.

Nine days later the Brigadier General in the US Air Force Reserve Charles F. Blair was buried with full military honours at Arlington National Cemetery, Washington D.C. In the 46 years of his military and commercial career, he had logged up ten million air miles over 45,000 flying hours. In that illustrious lifetime the pilot who had splashed down from the skies over Foynes in the county of Limerick, Ireland in 1942 was captain on 1,575 transatlantic crossings.

Bernard P McDonough: *Take-over tycoon to castle make-over king*

The President of the United States of America was coming to Ireland for a two day State visit in October 1970.

It was not only predictable but regarded as logical that the millionaire American industrialist behind the first luxury castle and a cluster of other hotels around Shannon Airport would want to be involved.

And that was how Bernard P McDonough had his name bandied around an Irish courtroom with suggestions that he had permitted an illegal bar when hosting the White House Press Corps elite of American journalism.

It could only happen in Ireland. But it came as no surprise that it happened to Bernard P McDonough.

Simultaneously he personified the American dream or a caricature straight out of the pages of the Harold Robins sagas of larger than life characters that played to their own individual rules in epic tales spanning generations.

He was the poor boy who rose from an unsettled childhood to include among his multiplicity of business deals a take-over of the company where he started working life at fifteen cents and hour. He was also the multi-millionaire in the rumpled tweed suit and battered hat who revelled in being mistaken as a member of the lower orders, who constantly tested the acumen loyalty and even the honesty of those around him and on one occasion simply bought a favourite hotel when it was unable to provide him with a room.

His grandfather and father were railroad men and when his mother died shortly after his birth in San Antonio in 1903, young Bernard and his sisters Julie and Catherine were placed in an orphanage while their father made arrangements for the children to be brought up by relatives. They joined their aunt Dehlia in Belpre, Ohio, across the Ohio river from Parkersburg, West Virginia where the principal industry was the Ames factory which produced shovels and hand tools.

"Never to be poor" was the pledge he made to himself in his teenage years. While still attending high school he was delivering the Parkersburg Sentinel in the morning and working late into the night lighting and snuffing out the street lights. In summer he worked in the oil fields with his towering 6ft 4inch uncle Pat and when he graduated he got his first job at the Ames factory.

The years until his mid-twenties were unsettled. He enrolled at Notre Dame University in South Bend, Indiana but dropped out after one year. He moved on to Georgetown University at Washington D.C. where he supported himself by driving a cab by night, but after he secured his law degree in 1925 he never practiced and tended to regard the legal fraternity with some suspicion.

He sold insurance, worked as a recruiter for a business school and also promoted membership of the American Automobile Association.

It was from his 1929 venture into construction that his business career took off and would keep on climbing. His breakthrough was a deal with Texaco Sun Oil and Standard Oil under which he built gas stations which he rented for ten years. The bank loan extended to acquire the lease on each gas station would be repaid in 8 years, so the final two years were clear profit and McDonough built 25 stations up and down the Ohio river.

He had married Alma Milhoan Spencer in 1938 and she would go on working as a grammar school teacher for three years until the arrival of Bernard McDonough III. By that time, Word War II conditions were creating an environment in which McDonough's free-wheeling style of deal making and instant response to opportunity could prosper. The construction industry was being restricted by a shortage of cement and concrete, so McDonough branched out into transportation and with a fleet of marine barges and by the end of 1945 became a supplier as well as a transporter when founding Houston Shell & Concrete and trucking to sites in war-surplus vehicles. For the next 20 years he would continue to buy up sand and gravel companies to consolidate his share of the market. But from 1950 onwards he moved into a different business league with the takeovers that established the McDonough reputation for turning around loss-making companies which saw his conglomerate corporation surge to a place in the Fortune magazine's listing of America's top 500 with total assets valued at $875million.

Two of the oldest industries in Parkersburg on the opposite side of the Ohio river to his adopted Belpre home were to come under his control. He bought into Parkersburg Rig and Reel makers of oil well drill rigs and pumping equipment. As chairman of the board in the post-war oil exploration boom he masterminded a merger that put the company on every oilfield in the United States and by 1954 he had secured a majority stake in the company. A year later he took control of the Ames firm which made the onetime 15-cents an hour employee the biggest producer of shovels in the world. Dating from 1774, the company that supplied steel shovels for the 1840s Gold Rush and the construction of the Union Pacific Railroad two decades later was at one time turning out more than one thousand different shovel models. The company had transplanted to Parkersburg in 1910 when it added garden tools to its production line but twenty years later its output was locked into the past and still producing hand tools for manual workers.

The razor sharp intelligence and instincts behind the judgement, timing and decisive action that gave McDonough the edge were not exclusively focused on business as he built up his empire and his fortune. He was conscious of his Irish ancestry and took some pride in the triumph of Ireland's Ronnie Delaney when winning the 1,500 metres at the Melbourne Olympics of 1956. But what intrigued McDonough was why Ireland's champion miler was training and running with an American university. He wanted to know why Ronnie Delaney spent most of his career in the USA running for his college, Villanova. The tycoon whose first college choice had been motivated by his ambition to play college football took his usual direct route to finding an answer. He made a call to a top sports magazine and learned that facilities to match the talent of Delaney and fellow athletes were not available talent back home in Ireland. He also learned that the Olympic hero was publicly lamenting that Ireland did not have a cinder track. It was the call of Ronnie Delaney rather than any sentimental attachment that brought Bernard McDonough to Ireland.

What happened next was entirely in character for Bernard P McDonough. Within a week he was on his way to Ireland. But he was not alone. The sports writer that he had consulted Gerald Holland was also brought along. They were heading for Dublin to see a man named Billy Morton who was the mainspring and spearhead of a campaign to add an athletics stadium to the facilities of the capital. It was again typical of McDonough that he had not sent any advance notice of his mission to Ireland or set up a meeting with Morton. He arrived in Dublin with his journalist aide only to discover that Morton was not in Dublin and not even in Ireland. The athletics zealot and promoter was in London. Adding another leg to his journey posed no problem to the millionaire. When he was in pursuit of a talent that he wanted to recruit, the millionaire was known to send an air ticket to his target and set up an interview in a city that both had to fly to. In that way he could keep the interview confidential and out of sight of those who might recognise either of them and it also tested how the target would respond to an opportunity that cropped up out of the blue.

Morton was tracked down and subjected to the McDonough brand of interrogation. But when he laid out his plans, McDonough signed a cheque for one thousand dollars. The enormity of that contribution is best measured in proportion to the fund-raising effort that Morton was leading. The fund had been launched by the Mayor of Dublin Robert Briscoe with a subscription of twenty five pounds. McDonough's dollars converted to more than five hundred pounds.

The McDonough gift was of breakthrough significance in bringing the stadium dream to reality. In recognition of his generosity, it was decided that a shovel from McDonough's Ames company would be used in breaking the ground for the sports stadium. McDonough reciprocated in his own inimitable fashion. The shovel that was shipped across the Atlantic was chromium-plated. And with it came a cheque for five thousand dollars.

McDonough now switched his sights to Galway where his grandparents had come from as impoverished peasants in the 1860s and, family fireside stories from his childhood told him, had walked to the port of Limerick where more than a quarter of a million Irish sailed to new and better tomorrows in the United States.

Determined to do something constructive that would improve the lot of the natives in the land of his ancestors, in the tightly-knit Ireland of the late 1950s stories abounded about the Yank with millions of dollars to spend who was scouting out possible investment opportunities. His name was mentioned in connection with a proposed multi-million furniture factory and there were genuine grounds to a report that he gave serious thought to setting up an Irish subsidiary of one of his American plants. But shortcomings in local infrastructure and transport services were identified even when preliminary checks were carried out. It did not help either that land prices seemed to increase once it became known that a rich American was in the frame. The upshot was a distinct cooling in McDonough's preference for Galway.

While he pondered various Irish investments and projects, McDonough continued to consolidate his business empire. He built up a one-third stake in a Kansas City competitor to his oilfields equipment firm with sights on a takeover, but withdrew when other bidders entered the fray. That was in 1959 and two years later he was adding to the reach of his construction interests with Gulf Coast Portland Cement which had 100 trucks operating out of 6 plants.

Because of his regular crossings of the Atlantic, McDonough became a familiar figure at Shannon Airport which was facing the threat of extinction as jet planes with no need for a re-fuelling stop came into the airline fleets in the 1960s. In the traditions of the hotel industry in which the airport supremo, Brendan O'Regan was steeped, Shannon made it its business to get to know its most regular travellers. And Brendan O'Regan

had made it his business to get to know Bernard P McDonough. On a June day in 1962 they were two men with two different problems. But within hours they were sharing not a problem but a mission that would bring startling change to the hotel and hospitality industry in Ireland.

It was a hotel in America that led to the meeting of minds between the two men when they talked on a June day at Shannon Airport in 1962.

As a transatlantic gateway operating from the start of commercial flights between the US and Europe, the vagueries and unpredictability of air travel were constants that the staff at Shannon Airport worked with and was the prime reason why the airport operated round the clock. That day Bernard McDonough was one of the passengers waiting for a delayed connection to the United States. In all such circumstances, dating from the day that he had spotted the celebrated Noel Coward left alone for three hours as he waited for a delayed flight, Brendan O'Regan had installed a smooth-running pubic relations machine to ensure that passengers did not depart with a poor impression of the airport. And Brendan O'Regan himself was looking after Bernard McDonough. He had good reason to do so. Because besides heading up the airport

Sales & Catering Service, O'Regan was also the chairman of the Irish Tourist Board and had been entrusted with a new government mandate to lure the jets down from the skies with path finding tourism and industrial development around the airport.

O'Regan had been encouraging McDonough to set up a plant to manufacture ball bearings, but the project was foundering.

"What about a hotel then?" suggested O'Regan to which McDonough responded –"what kind of hotel?"

O'Regan mentioned the new Shannon Shamrock Inn that had been built in record time and opened for business in August 1959 for American investor Al McCarthy. O'Regan had very personal involvement with that development as he had bought the site in the shadow of Bunratty Castle specifically to accommodate the type of hotel he had noted during his visits to the United States.

McDonough was not impressed with the suggestion and felt that bringing Ireland up to date with the preferences of American travellers warranted something more lavish.

This time it was O'Regan who asked the question. "What kind of hotel do you mean?"

"Something like the Greenbrier," McDonough said naming a favourite luxury hotel at White Sulphur Springs in his home state of West Virginia.

He most probably did not expect it, but O'Regan was familiar with the Greenbrier. He had been there as one of four Irish representatives in a group of 16 from Europe who were selected to spend 6 weeks in the United States under the Marshall Plan regeneration programme for post-war rebuilding of the broken economics of Europe. They had been taken to the most popular resorts, hotels and leisure facilities of the USA to acquaint them with the standards that American travellers would be looking for when they took their vacations in Europe.

Taking his cue from their mutual regard for the American hotel, O'Regan said that he knew just the property that would suit as a hotel to match the Greenbrier.

At this stage in the conversation, the two men were virtually reading each other's minds as

McDonough answered – "is it Dromoland Castle?"

"How did you know?" O'Regan enquired.

"The taxi driver told me," the millionaire said.

Neither man was known to hesitate when opportunity came knocking. As McDonough had several hours to wait for his flight, on O'Regan's suggestion they drove straight to Dromoland where Lord Inchiquin, Sir Donough O'Brien had been alerted that a potential buyer was on the way.

The descendants of Brian Boru, the 11th century High King and conqueror of the Danes had moved their seat from Lemenagh Castle on the edge of the Burren country of county Clare in 1686 and had taken the ornamental stone gateway with them when they moved to Dromoland.

Lord Inchiquin met McDonough and O'Regan in his study which was located immediately inside the front door of the castle and would become the lounge bar.

The meeting ran smoothly but then gained pace and began to move too fast.

When the asking price was raised, Lord Inchiquin replied that he was offering the castle and 300 acres of the 2,000 acre estate for fifty thousand pounds (then Ireland was on the same currency as England).

"I'll take it," the American deal maker said.

Lord Inchiquin began a conducted tour of the castle, but announced that he had changed his mind about the area of land to be included in the package. Now it was to be 100 acres and not 300 acres.

"But you said 300 acres," a suddenly uneasy McDonough pointed out.

Lord Inchiquin explained that he had become confused in negotiating in dollars against the value of the pound. With the dollar valued at around a third of a pound at the time, the price being quoted came to roughly fifty thousand dollars.

But McDonough wanted to do business in terms of the original deal and asked what the revised cost would be for 300 acres.

Lord Inchiquin wanted one hundred pounds per acre which would add twenty thousand pounds or around sixty thousand dollars to the asking price.

"Out of the question," McDonough snapped and departed for the airport.

Then, as he would throughout his decades in the topmost echelons of State administration in Ireland, Brendan O'Regan was a peace maker. Back at Shannon Airport he telephoned Lord Inchiquin in a last ditch effort to rescue the sale. What he got was an offer that would grant hunting and fishing rights on the entire 2,000 acres of the Dromoland estate in return for parting with 300 rather than 100 acres.

Lord Inchiquin agreed.

"I'll think about it" said McDonough who was already in his seat on the flight back to America.

A few weeks later Brendan O'Regan was in New York ostensibly on other business but telephoned McDonough and asked if he was still considering the purchase of Dromoland. "I may buy it," he said and invited O'Regan to join him in Parkersburg. McDonough was waiting for O'Regan when he landed at Parkersburg Airport and announced –"I bought the place over the phone".

Brendan O'Regan's exceptional connections back in Ireland were put to use during his stay as McDonough's guest. Over dinner with his guest the new American lord of Dromoland looked for guidance on engaging a solicitor to handle legal matters on the Irish end of his interests. When a name was recommended, even though it was Sunday, McDonough asked O'Regan to call the solicitor straight away and when the connection was made, the solicitor received immediate instructions to get hold of the title deeds of Dromoland Castle.

The same McDonough way of getting things done applied as Americans were drafted in to manage all the activities that turned the ancient and in some places crumbling castle into a luxury hotel. Architect Bill Trautwein was only starting in his own practice when he was called in to remodel the porch on McDonough's old home. He was not over excited about the commission but changed his tune when told that a company aircraft would be sent to pick him up. Thereafter he found himself working on a series of commissions for one of the most powerful industrialists in the United States. McDonough called him to say he had bought Dromoland and wanted the architect to look it over. "When would you like to have me over?" the architect enquired.

"Tonight," said McDonough.

The architect was followed by a pair of American engineers to oversee the remodeling of the castle and a man named Don Spencer who was sent in to supervise the re-decoration of the castle. He had been given a budget of seventy thousand pounds to cover the decoration but found that a great number of the castle windows needed to be replaced and that work alone consumed the funds earmarked for decoration.

In the refurbishment of Dromoland, McDonough knew what he wanted because he knew what he liked. He liked the Greenbrier Hotel in his home state and he knew that hotel had been decorated by the Dorothy Draper Company in New York. So he headed there and announced that he had bought an old Irish castle and wanted it decorated. The man who jumped at the chance was Carlton Varney who would be involved for decades with Dromoland and with an outlet of his own in the nearby village of Newmarket-on-Fergus.

Even the wallpaper came from the United States as large shipments of light fittings and other fixtures were brought to Dromoland. Four hundred locals were taken on at wages that were well above the local rates so that central heating and every other comfort was installed to transform Dromoland Castle into a 20th century palace of luxury and a showpiece that would put the west of Ireland into elite publications and media just as Brendan O'Regan was spearheading the drive to bring new life to Ireland through Shannon Airport. Dromoland Castle opened as a hotel in June 1963 right on schedule. But Bernard McDonough was far from finished with hotel operations in Ireland.

Dromoland Castle Hotel as an Irish match for the best in the world and another trail blazer for Shannon ticked another of the boxes on the Brendan O'Regan action agenda. Bunratty Castle had been restored and had rapidly become a brand name in its American appeal; the American Al had been charmed into building the Shannon Shamrock Hotel and Dromoland made up the set. It would come as no surprise to Bernard McDonough that Brendan O'Regan had other plans for the partnership they had formed between Irish State innovation and American private enterprise.

Dromoland was putting Ireland and Shannon especially on the map in terms of luxury tourism and was serving a key dual-purpose for Shannon as an eye-opening haven of luxury for the prospecting multinationals that were dropping in to look over Shannon as a location for industrial investment.

As they sat down to first class cuisine under the portraits personifying the pedigree of the castle or settled into their four poster beds, globe-trotting industrialists were not only satisfied that Shannon knew how to make its newcomers welcome, it was also laying on the top of the range facilities that major corporations would demand when entertaining.

It was not a one way street however. While Dromoland was illustriously serving the purpose for Shannon, Shannon was reciprocating by putting much of the weight of its promotion campaigns and hospitality budgets behind Dromoland. The twin O'Regan headed agencies of Shannon Development and the Sales & Catering Service at the airport were directing business to Dromoland and the high-performance Shannon publicity and public relations machine in New York was not just promoting Dromoland as the latest touch of class adorning Shannon but also sending a stream of publicists to Dromoland. That the Dromoland owner had high regard for the polished skills of the Shannon and an expert eye

in spotting the right talent was borne out when he poached Patricia (Pat) Barry from the Shannon promotion team and brought her to Dromoland where she came in to head up public relations but would rise to the top as general manager.

With McDonough hooked on Shannon and what it was going about, Brendan O'Regan told him of his ambition to see a hotel located within the precincts of Shannon Airport. Typically, there was more than one objective to the project. The prime purpose was to provide regular hotel accommodation in place of "The Camp", a cluster of wooden chalets that formed what was virtually a village community of airport workers and also ready-made accommodation for passengers forced to overnight when flights were delayed or held up by technical trouble. The second objective was to provide home for the Shannon College of Hotel Management that O'Regan had set up in 1951 as yet another pioneering first in Ireland. Consistent with the giant jigsaw of interlocking initiatives that made up the big Shannon picture of O'Regan's vision, there were multiple benefits to go round. The hotel college had evolved from the airport kitchens where the enormous output of meals for consumption in the air by the flying layer of society that could afford the privilege demanded superior cuisine. The Shannon restaurants had established a prestige international reputation and almost from the start in 1945, "Shannon training" was a badge of quality in the catering trade. With Shannon established as a career springboard for chefs and restaurant staff, the hotel college was a natural progression. The pronounced advantage for Bernard McDonough's second hotel came with the hotel college students who staffed the kitchens, restaurant, bar and the other departments of the hotel operation for the greater part of the year. So it happened that the bulk of the staff at what was named the International Hotel consisted of the future elite of Ireland's hotel industry and graduates who rose to eminent heights with the great chains and leaders in their field in the rest of the world. With the college students delivering their best efforts to satisfy college lecturers and supervisors, lunch at the International Hotel was one of the delights in the perks of airport managers and a surprise for first-time visitors.

Following less than a year after Dromoland, the International Hotel provided a close-up of Bernard McDonough style of management which had already become local legend around Dromoland. In the same vein as his US-based operations, he changed his top people almost at random and with little apparent thought about their qualifications other than his instincts that they were the right fit for the job he had in mind.

All facets of the McDonough brand of people management were seen in the earliest working years of Barbara de Lacy, daughter and only child of a prominent Limerick city businessman and an athlete who was a legend in his own lifetime.

Although she had followed in her father's running shoes as an invincible on track and field, Barbara had a sheltered upbringing that did not quite prepare her for her first summer job. She had just finished secondary school and was still weighing up her future course in life when her first encounter with the world of work coincided with the summer of 1964 opening of the International Hotel. Neither the novice nor the hotel were ready.

Her first surprise was to find that the hotel was located on what was still a building site and, having been outfitted with her uniform, that was followed by the shock of what amounted to bedlam at the hotel.

"The hotel reception area was in what appeared to be uproar. The head lady was struggling to bring order to the place and asked me who I was. When I said I was the new junior receptionist, she said –"Thank God you are here" and turning to the switchboard behind the reception desk, directed –"you can look after this," Barbara recalls.

More than 40 years on as Barbara de Lacy Hartigan, a leading water colours painter, the terror and trauma of her introduction to paid employment are still etched deep in her memory.

"I don't recall if I had even seen a switchboard before but I certainly had no idea how to operate the contraption that in those days was a big panel with what appeared to be dozens of cables dangling out of it. With nobody to show me how, it was a crash course in learning by trial and error, with most of the trials inflicted on the hotel guests and people trying to have incoming calls connected. I distinctly remember a titled lady guest in the hotel who was waiting to make contact with a baron but my efforts only connected her to the kitchen and then the laundry before I gave up in panic and pulled all the cables out of the switchboard. I cried my way through every day of my first week."

But that was only a prelude to her first impressions of her American millionaire employer.

Her first brush with the millionaire owner of the hotel was over the telephone lines. "I had somehow mastered the intricacies of the switchboard when I took an incoming call from a gentleman with an American accent." When she went through the standard routine of asking who was calling, the voice on the other end interjected - "You are not to say who shall I say is speaking". That rebuke was just for starters.

The teenager was still getting the hang of things after about two weeks in the job and was working the 7 o'clock morning shift when the industrialist materialised in front of the reception desk. "He was not at all what I imagined a millionaire would look like. He was dressed in what was non-descript clothes and he tended to twitch.

"Where is Julian?" he asked.
I explained that the manager, Mr. Chapman, did not start until later in the day.

"I'll wait," the owner said, taking a seat opposite the reception desk.

"Gimme Tony Murphy," he ordered.

Barbara was at a complete loss as to who Tony Murphy was and where he might be located when another lady on the staff sprang to her aid –"that would be Tony Murphy in Cork".

Even with that guidance she ran into difficulties. "I had no idea which of the many Tony Murphys listed in the telephone directory he wanted to contact, so I asked for guidance.

"My God, you stupid Irish. Just forget it," the owner growled.

Not for the first time Bernard McDonough's brusque reprimands to his staff at all levels took place in public.

"I was shattered as his outburst occurred in front of a hall filled with hotel patrons," Barbara Hartigan recalled. "That was another day of crying. But Mr. Chapman came along and comforted me ".

"Don't worry. That's how he is," the manager confided.

But very soon and possibly at the prompting of Julian Chapman, Barbara also got to know the other side of Bernard McDonough. She was spending some free time back home to Limerick city when she received a phone call from a hotel colleague who whispered –"you are going to get a call from Mr. McDonough".

While the hotel junior waited in trepidation for the call, soon afterwards the call came through and the voice at the other end said –"This is Bernard".

He had initially tried to contact her at the International Hotel which was how Barbara got the advance warning of the call and the purpose of the call to her home was to ask when she was due back behind the reception desk. "Tomorrow at 3 o'clock" she answered.

From a perspective of more than 40 years, Barbara recalled –"Mr. McDonough probably sensed my anxiety at the other end of the line and he quickly banished my fears".

"I'm going to send Johnny Madden to collect you and he will bring you over to Dromoland. You are going to come to dinner" she was told. John Madden was the young assistant manager that McDonough had poached from the new Shannon Shamrock Hotel to beef up the

Dromoland staff. In fact he did not come to collect Barbara. Instead she was picked up by a taxi and driven to Dromoland where John Madden joined the owner and one of his thousands of employees at dinner".

"What do you think of this place?" the owner eventually enquired of his young guest. When she replied that it was like fairyland, he said – "Maybe next year you would like to work here".

Over the next two years the art college student had a summer job as part of the reception desk team at Dromoland Castle. There she had a front row view of the comings and goings of celebrities, bluebloods, statesmen, dignatories from all walks of life, and business moguls. She also had first hand experience of the unorthodox ways in which Mr. McDonough tested the efficiency, loyalty and honesty of his staff.

The whims and at times quirky behaviour of the millionaire owner would startle guests as much as management and staff and become legend in the hotel trade. When a meal did not come up to his expectations, it was not unknown for McDonough to announce to guests in the Dromoland dining room that there would be no charge for their meal. In such cases, turnover of chefs and other staff in the kitchens and dining room of Dromoland was often brisk.

When in residence, the Dromoland owner would also set tests for the hotel staff. He would randomly select a bedroom where he would remove a bulb from a lamp. The member of the housekeeping staff who checked and found that the bulb was missing could receive a hundred dollar bill as a reward. He was also known to deliberately drop litter around the grounds and again check that staff took action to keep the estate in pristine condition.

Even though he had taken to her after their Dromoland dinner, the future Mrs. Barbara Hartigan was not exempt from the challenges and tests that Dromoland staff constantly faced.

"One day Mr. McDonough engaged me in conversation for a while as he sat with me in the hotel reception area," Barbara recalled. "When he stood and departed I noticed that there was a US currency bill close to the chair where he had been sitting. I had been cautioned like all other Dromoland staff that Mr. McDonough had his own special ways of testing his employees, so I knew what to do. It was a one hundred dollar bill which amounted to a very considerable sum of money and probably worth a month's wages in the Ireland of the early 1960s. I placed the bill in an envelope with a note explaining the find to Mr. McDonough and suggesting that he may have dropped it."

Some time later he returned to the reception desk with the envelope in hand.
"He plucked out the one hundred dollar bill. He did not explain himself or give any hint that the bill had been deliberately placed to test my honesty," Barbara added.

"So you found the hundred dollar bill," he commented.

He then handed the bill to the receptionist and said casually – "I'm sure you can make use of it".

At Dromoland the natural artistic flair of the young receptionist was recognised when she was put in charge of flower arranging and would rise in the misty dawns to gather flowers in the walled garden and pluck lilies and greenery from the lake. Forty years later, Barbara Hartigan delivered her verdict on her experiences with Bernard McDonough. "Those Dromoland summers opened up a new world for me that none but a handful of people in Ireland of the time had experienced. For me Dromoland was a most wonderful finishing school".

A third McDonough hotel within the take-off path of Shannon Airport was on the way when the owner acquired a hotel back on his American home ground which was to be linked up to the Irish operations.

The addition to the Irish hotel operations was The Clare Inn which was being built on part of the Dromoland Castle estate. That hotel was underway in 1967 when McDonough was involved in his latest take-over of a loss-maker that he had identified as having the potential to be whipped into shape and turned around. He was in Phoenix Arizona to buy the famous meat packers, Cudahy Packaging when he came up against a problem that he seldom encountered in the United States and never in Ireland. He wished to stay at the Casa Blanca Inn at Scottsdale but there was no vacancy. So he bought the property and the hotel became a training ground for the Irish hotels until it was sold to the Ramada Inn chain in 1971.

The Clare Inn opened for business in 1968 and was followed by a sister hotel, the Limerick Inn.

But while the Limerick Inn was located on the fringe of Limerick city, it was nevertheless just inside the border of county Clare where the planners of the local county council were to get involved in a stand off with the American hotelier.

The plans submitted for the Limerick Inn provided that the fire escape was to be located inside the hotel building. But the planners decreed otherwise. They wanted the fire escape to be an external structure. Bernard McDonough did not agree. Without full planning permission, the completed hotel property could not get a hotel licence and therefore could not operate. So be it was the attitude of the owner and the latest of the new hotels in the Shannon area stood idle on the road between Limerick and Shannon Airport.

Then came the visit of President Richard Nixon to Ireland in October 1970 and the repercussions that brought the planning row between the American millionaire and the local council into the national headlines.

It was during what should have been quite normal court proceedings and the hearing of an application for a licence for what was described as "the luxury Limerick Inn" that the matter of the hotel operating illegally was brought into the open. And it was brought up by the presiding judge of the Circuit Court.

Due to the impasse between the owner and the planning authority, the matter of the licence for the Limerick Inn had been cropping up in the court on a number of occasions. So important was the matter that a prior application had been brought as a matter of urgency before Judge Barra O Briain at a hearing in his Enniskerry home on the Wicklow outskirts of Dublin where a decision was adjourned.

When the hotel licence application resurfaced at Limerick Circuit Court in mid-October 1970, the judge interrupted the formal application to enquire how it had come about that the Limerick Inn had functioned since the previous application and the adjourning of a court decision.

By way of explanation, the barrister acting for the hotel, Dan O'Keeffe, told the court that it was his understanding that the Limerick Inn was operating as a hotel but without a licence to sell liquor that a hotel licence provided for. But the judge pointed out that there had been newspaper reports that suggested that drink had in fact been served in the hotel during the visit of President Nixon.

Making a point that "there was no means by which drink could be served without a licence", the judge said he wanted evidence as to whether drink had been sold.

The law agent for the Clare County Council planning authority weighed in by telling the court that he had read reports in which it had been stated that "exorbitant prices" were charged for drink served in the bar of the Limerick Inn during the presidential visit.

The case attained an even high profile at the next hearing when the McDonough hotel introduced as a witness the nationally prominent Brendan O'Regan, who was then chairman of Bord Failte (the Irish Tourist Board) as well as the dual supremo at Shannon as head of the airport's Sales and Catering Service and founder chairman of the Shannon Free Airport Development Company.

Arising from that hearing, which was also adjourned, Judge Barra O Briain referred at the follow-up court session to "an arrangement stated to have been made to sell drink at an unlicensed hotel on the occasion of President Nixon's visit".

The judge added that evidence to the previous hearing had "strongly suggested the probability of drink having been sold to the (White House) Press Corps" during the presidential visit.

Judge Barra O Briain was scathing in his pronouncement on the matter, stating – "the visit of any person, however eminent or privileged, to this country cannot abrogate or suspend the laws of Ireland. This is or should be axiomatic". The judge voiced his reservations that to grant the application for a licence "would be to make a court order that would form the basis for an illegal act" and added –"to have sold drink was conduct which might amount to unfitness or misconduct".

That hearing in the first week of November 1970 again adjourned the matter of the hotel licence application but was back on the court list two weeks later when Bernard McDonough finally conceded on the fire escape issue.

By way of explanation which might also be regarded as covering the illegal sale of drink controversy, a statement from the hotel owner stated –"I respect Ireland's laws and have always conformed with them. But we believe and are confirmed in this belief by our insurance people in the United States that enclosing a fire escape would create a hazardous situation for our guests".

The court proceedings to bring the Limerick Inn into line with the conditions of the planning permission were adjourned yet again. The wrangle was settled in 1971 and the issue of the illegal serving and sale of drink when the White House Press Corps was staying at the hotel quietly slipped into oblivion.

While McDonough was dealing with the opening actions of what became a war of words with the planners over the Limerick Inn fire escape, he was engrossed on the other side of the Atlantic in his biggest ever take over. He had fixed his sights on Endicott Johnson, footwear makers whose hold on the work-shoe and young people's footwear market had been on the slide for some time. A giant in American manufacturing and retail, Endicott Johnson at its height was turning out 45,000,000 pairs of shoes per year from 29 factories which employed part of the 19,000 workforce which extended to stores across the United States. All time loses of twelve million dollars in 1961 when output had fallen to 29 million pairs of shoes were followed by years of savage cuts. Bernard McDonough started to buy into the company in 1967 and built up his stake during an acrimonious power struggle to emerge with majority control in January 1969.

The wheeler dealer in McDonough showed itself again in Ireland when he was juggling with options in relation to the troublesome Limerick Inn. At one stage he offered to swop the hotel for the Carrigoran convent and nursing home near Newmarket-on-Fergus and not far from Dromoland Castle. His idea was for a direct switch which would see the Limerick Inn converted to an ultra-modern nursing home and for Carrigoran to follow Dromoland in a transformation to a hotel. But second thoughts scuppered the deal. In what was almost a repeat of the reservations which had almost killed off the Dromoland purchase, McDonough wanted the convent farm to be included in the transaction. It was a deal too far for the Irish Sisters of the Incarnate Word. Instead the Limerick Inn was sold to local hotelier, Tom Ryan who owned the Two Mile Inn directly across the road from the Limerick Inn.

With the Endicott Johnston take over making McDonough the biggest producer of shovels and footwear in the United States, his McDonough Company involving building materials and hand tools went public in 1970. Earnings grew in every year so that twelve months before its 1981 sale to Hanson Trust of Great Britain the combined turnover of McDonough enterprises came to four hundred and fifty million dollars and 1980 profits of twenty one and a half million dollars.

The International Hotel at Shannon was sold in October 1982 to the Aer Rianta airports authority which set down a diversification seed which would see that State body take over and rebuild the troubled Great Southern Hotel chain which had faltered under the ownership of the State transport company, C.I.E.

Bernard P McDonough died in October 1985 and his memory was perpetuated in the following year when his widow Alma gifted five and a half million dollars to fund the Bernard P McDonough Centre for Leadership and Business at Marietta College in his native Ohio. In the following year, the McDonough era in shaping the Irish hotel industry came to an end when Dromoland Castle and its neighbouring Clare Inn were sold.

Mark and Lavone Andrews: *Woman's touch revives dream castle*

When Mark Edwin Andrews, Texas attorney and oilman with business interests across a wide spectrum of activity, passed away in his native Houston in August, 1992, the distinguished congregation at the funeral service would have been curious about two of the eight pallbearers.

The attendance at the Episcopalian Church of St. John the Divine would have reflected the family pedigree and the outstanding career that spanned law, the academic world, business, wartime naval service and government service. Marking his distinction as the first Navy man to be appointed Assistant Secretary of the Navy, government and military were prominent at the funeral service. Reverend Laurens A. Hall, Rector at St. John the Divine officiated and was assisted by Reverend John Harper, Rector of St. John's at Lafayette Square in Washington D.C. The U.S. Navy conducted a military ceremony following the graveside service at Glenwood Cemetery.

There were eight pallbearers and twelve honorary pallbearers. Among the familiar names of commerce, law and government from Texas who were named as pallbearers were Flan Gleeson from the village of Sixmilebridge in the west of Ireland and Paddy O'Grady who lived a few miles down the road in county Clare.

Flan Gleeson and Paddy O'Grady were the connection to a castle in Ireland and a boyhood daydream that was fulfilled when Mark Edwin Andrews and his architect wife, Lavone brought a forlorn Irish castle back to life to resound again to music, song and the boisterous feasting of guests in the upsurge of American tourism to Ireland which sprang from Shannon Airport.

The boy was taken on a trip to Europe during a vacation from his education in public and private schools in Houston and New Jersey. In company with his parents Jesse and Celeste, their transatlantic liner made a call at the Cobh (Queenstown) port which gave the travellers their first sighting of land on the edge of to Europe. It was from the deck of the liner that the imagination of the young Mark Edwin was captivated by the sight of an ancient castle. At that time he imagined himself as a knight or heroic champion defending the castle but it was the thought of having a castle of his own that stayed with him right through his Princeton years and the studies at graduate school at the University of Colorado and the South Texas College of Law where he was first in his graduation class of 1934. By that time he had married his first wife and was already making his way in the business world. For four years from age 25 he worked with the B.C. Andrews cotton exporting firm of Dallas and in the two years leading to his law degree he was President of the Andrews, Loop & Co. cotton exporting company.

Mark Edwin followed his father into law practice and also into the management of large oil properties in Texas and Louisiana and was an independent oil producer as President of Westmoreland Manufacturing Company from 1936 until America entered World War II.

The distinctions and successes that marked his academic and business careers were replicated in the U.S. Navy. With an early promotion to the office of the Secretary of the Navy he was in charge of purchasing aircraft and engines for the Navy and by the end of the war was head of Navy Ship Procurement. A year later he succeeded Vice Admiral Walter Buck as Chief of Procurement which put him in charge of all Navy procurement. He was assigned to write the post-war procurement legislation which endured into the age of space exploration as the law under which the US Department of Defence made its contracts. He was awarded the Legion of Merit in 1946, the year in which he published his first book "Building a Navy" and a year later he became the first naval officer to be named Assistant Secretary of the Navy.

When he returned to civilian life and independent oil production in 1949, he had married for the second time. He had been married for 18 years to his first wife, Marguerite McLellan of Princeton when she passed away in June 1946. Also marrying for the second time was his wife Lavone Dickensheets, a Texas native and architect. She became Mrs. Andrews in 1948 while her new husband was Assistant Secretary of the Navy and returned with him to Houston and the oil business. Together they built up the Ancon Oil and Gas private energy company where Mark Edwin was President and his wife Vice President continuously from 1957. Mr. Andrews also acquired control of and reorganized the Dixel Manufacturing Company where he was Chairman of the Board from 1961 to 1965.

The Andrews family loved to travel and with their son, Mark, they ventured as far as Russia, Egypt and the Holy Land. It was on the return leg of a trip that they set foot in Ireland for the first time and the prospect of having a castle as a home was resurrected.

As Lavone Andrews recalled in a 1994 lecture, they were driving around the head of Galway Bay and suddenly, pointing to a small square tower at the water's edge, her husband said to his son – "There Mark. Wouldn't it be fun to have one of those?"

As Mrs. Andrews recalled it, her son's response was "oh yes!" while her reaction was "ugh!"

While family opinion seemed to be divided on the issue, the thought of a castle in Ireland stayed in the forefront of Mark Edwin's mind. So much so that when they made the acquaintance of a man whose business was in overseas property deals, Mark Edwin recalled their sighting of the Galway castle and asked to be kept in mind if any property of its type came up for sale.

A matter of weeks later, they got a message "your castle is for sale. Would you like to go see it?"

With son Mark gone away to boarding school mother was missing him. That the parents were ready to embrace anything that would turn their minds to something new and different was evidenced when they got word that their Galway castle was being offered for sale. They took off for Ireland the next day.

As with many aspects of Ireland, things did not turn out exactly as they expected.

First of all it was not the same castle although it was in the vicinity of Galway Bay. It also transpired that the elderly widow and member of the British aristocracy who owned the castle did want to sell but wished to remain on as the castle tenant.

This setback only served to strengthen the resolve of Mark Edwin Andrews to have a castle in Ireland. Over the next two weeks he and his wife covered over 2,000 miles and found their way to numerous ruins and remnants of the castles that punctuate the Irish countryside. But none came up to expectations.

They finally decided to go the official route and headed for Dublin and the residence of the US Ambassador to Ireland. The racehorse-owning Raymond Guest also happened to be an acquaintance. He directed the Texan couple to the National Monuments division of government where they got further directions to retrace their steps. When the couple expressed their preference for a castle in the west of Ireland, they were told that the man to see was Brendan O'Regan.

O'Regan had been described to them as "Mister West of Ireland". But he was a great deal more than that because besides building a sales empire with high profits and high employment around Shannon Airport, his flair in originating the first Duty Free Store in the world had also brought him to the top of the tourism tree as chairman of the Irish Tourist Board.

Brendan O'Regan not only took the Andrews around to view a number of castles but he also showed them what could be done with a castle near Shannon Airport. Almost from the opening of Shannon Airport in 1945, O'Regan had harboured the idea of restoring the great 15th century Bunratty Castle which stood roofless and lifeless as he drove past each day. He had included the idea in a submission on priorities for building a tourism industry which he put to government in 1950. In 1965 he was able to not only show the Andrews what had come about but they were also able to experience what had been achieved.

In the 1950s, Lord Gort, the heir to the old Irish title, had come over to Ireland with the intention of buying the ancestral seat of Lough Cutra Castle on the fringe of the town of Gort. But Brendan O'Regan had other ideas. Through the Irish art and antiquities expert John Hunt, he knew that Lord Gort had assembled a collection of medieval furnishings and artifacts. Because Bunratty Castle stood as the finest example of its type in Ireland or Britain, O'Regan persuaded Lord Gort to buy the castle and join with the government and the tourist board in faithfully restoring the castle as the historically appropriate home for the Gort collection.

The Andrews also saw for themselves what O'Regan and his Shannon mission had done when they were his guests at the Bunratty banquet. In its first year the Bunratty Medieval Banquet had been offered free along with a tour to any transatlantic traveller who stopped off at Shannon for 24 hours. This offer, along with free overnight accommodation at the 200-beds cluster of chalets where air crews and on-call airport staff stayed, helped to establish Shannon as a tourist destination. By 1965 when the Andrews sampled the Bunratty experience, the castle banquet and entertainment had become synonymous with Ireland in the US travel market. So much so that the castle banquet was considered the ideal introduction or farewell to a vacation in Ireland.

A whole new scenario opened up for the Andrews and their quest for a castle in Ireland. Brendan O'Regan suggested that rather than the tower castles or tower houses that they had been viewing they should instead think about a larger property which could be restored like Bunratty and help pay its way by becoming a sister castle extension of the medieval banquet operation.

From Brendan O'Regan's point of view, the couple from Texas could not have made a more timely appearance. He explained that because of the enormous success of the Bunratty banquet, demand was running ahead of capacity in the peak months of the year and he had been searching for an additional castle venue to take the overflow. He had found a castle ruin in what he regarded as the right setting and had been trying for some time to raise the money for its purchase and restoration. He had even held discussions with an Irish architect who he considered right for the restoration job. But a matter of weeks before the Andrews came on the scene, the architect had died suddenly.

"Now, out of the blue we had appeared with a built-in architect and a desire to buy and restore a castle. No less than a miracle," Lavone Andrews recalled almost 30 years later.

They were taken to see Knappogue Castle which had endured for most of 500 years but only fell into dereliction in the thirty years or so since Ireland had achieved independence. The castle had survived occupation during the Cromwellian suppression and had also been spared in the widespread destruction of great houses identified with the landlord classes during the War of Independence. Knappogue had a Gaelic pedigree and was one of the many castles built by the McNamara earls of Thomond. The castle's historic significance was recognised when the republican Clare County Council convened a meeting there.

The sight that met their eyes was recalled in detail by Mrs. Andrews in her 1994 lecture.

"There it stood, a great pile of grey stone towering above a bleak bare landscape, very cold, very silent with two great blackbirds floating in and out of the gaping holes where windows had been. There was no sign of a roof anywhere; no windows; no doors; no floors. Not one speck of wood, lead, glass or anything else but stone and not all of the stone. And the land around had been stripped of trees".

On this occasion it was Mark Edwin Andrews who shuddered. But Knappogue reached out to Lavone Andrews. "The strangest thing happened to me," she recorded. "I had resisted the idea of owning a castle in Ireland every step of the way. And here I was, standing in front of a very forbidding ruin, shivering in the wild cold wind, but absolutely overwhelmed by the conviction that the whole thing was meant to be".

She turned to her husband and said –"Well Edwin, if you want a castle in Ireland, this is the one". Decades later she confessed –"When I look back I can't image how I came to say such a thing. But we went straight ahead without hesitation".

The castle of Knappogue had been through a number of incarnations since 1467 when it first loomed up on the territory of Thomond as a fortified tower house in the style of the Normans who marked the territories brought under their sway with a chain of strategically sited sentinel towers. The castle had been altered and extended in the 17th, 18th and 19th centuries and stood as a stone representation of the architectural styles of each period.

Restoration of the multi-faceted castle was going to demand a very special architect. In Lavone Dickensheets Andrews, Knappogue found an architectural fairy godmother who would conjure up the magic to bring out the best in a Cinderella castle and bring it back to its rightful regal standing.

Born in the Jefferson county seat of Beaumont, Lavone was named after her mother. Her father, Charles Dickensheets, was a newspaper reporter sent from the east coast to cover the Texas oil boom and became part of the story himself when forsaking journalism to join the oil strikes stakes.

Opting for architecture after schooling in San Francisco and Los Angeles, Lavone Dickensheets proved her mettle in what was a male-dominated profession. She was one of a hundred students who enrolled for the architectural programme at Houston's Rice Institute in 1929 but six years later was one of only five who received their 1935 graduate degrees – and the only woman.

With licence number 413 from the State of Texas to practice as an architect, Lavone aimed for an apprenticeship with the best architect she could find, joining the firm headed by the noted architect John Staub where she stayed until 1938 when she opened her own office.

Her first assignment was for a one-storey house and while residential properties were to be the backbone of the early years, she expanded into other areas and into completely new territories for an architect when World War II came along. She worked on the conversion of a machine shop into a gun barrel plant plus wartime warehousing and installation of heavy duty equipment. During his Washington D.C. wartime service in the office of the Secretary of the Navy, she married Mark Edwin and while they combined to build their Ancon Oil and Gas venture on their return to Houston, Lavone continued her architectural practice. She designed vegetable oil refineries, schools and office buildings and had completed work on a Houston health centre when Knappogue Castle came into their lives.

Nobody was under any illusions about the enormity of the task that lay ahead. But even getting started had its unexpected complications for two Texans wanting to buy a castle and part of the land around it. What had been the castle estate had been divided up by a Land Commission set up by the fledgling new Irish Free State and the lands passed to locals who had not previously owned their own land. As a result, Mrs. Andrews would recall in later years "the land was sold almost by the square inch and it was almost like getting pieces of the farmer himself".

Acquiring the land around the castle and the strips of property flanking the avenue entrance became very complicated because written into the sale were provisions for future development and use of the castle and lands. It took months and the Andrews confessed that without the involvement of Brendan O'Regan and his Shannon Development company the deal would have had no chance.

It took months of delicately balanced negotiations to complete the purchase but the

Andrews made the most of the time and made for themselves a temporary base on the property beside the ruined castle they had bought.

The chatter in pub and general store of the locals in the area around Quin in county Clare centred on the American oilman who had been a top figure in Washington D.C. and his wife who were spending most of their time in what Ireland of the mid-1960s called a caravan and was normally sited at a beach for summertime vacations.

To the Andrews it was not a caravan or what they would call a trailer back in Texas. It was their office and the nerve-centre for the restoration of Knappogue. An architect's drawing board for Lavone to work at was the top priority but not far behind was a stove because the Andrews were going to spend a great deal of time outdoors - every inch of Knappogue Castle had to be measured.

The central Norman-era tower of the castle stood over one hundred feet high with walls twelve feet in thickness. The central tower conformed to the standard Norman castles that are seen in all parts of Ireland. While serving as a residence for a member of the nobility, its primary purpose was protective. Consequently the tower was a forbidding prospect to the attacker, the bulging stone walls were sturdy but inside the character was austere and the comforts few.

Like countless others in Ireland that followed in the Norman style, the original tower core of Knappogue rose in three levels and accommodated four large and three small rooms.

At ground level, entry was through a door in the east wall facing a spiral staircase which coiled left to give a retreating defender the advantage by giving him the upper hand in swordplay. Opposite the stairs was a small room for the guard and behind was a large room with a wooden-floor loft where hay and grain would be stored and where cattle, swine and their herdsmen took refuge when the castle was threatened.

Only an earthen floor remained on the lowest level, but an early bonus in the restoration work was the black marble staircase rising to the top of the castle which had survived in the stone shell that had otherwise been stripped of everything that could be torn up, torn out and moved. The intact staircase also saved a great deal of calculations because by measuring each riser the overall height of the original castle could be worked out.

On the second level was a large vaulted room which also had a wooden loft which served as the quarters for the castle fighting men and their families.

At the top was the great hall in which the lord of the manor and his family resided. A high beamed ceiling supported by heavy wooden trusses would have been roofed with thatch with a lantern-type opening through which smoke from the central hearth in the great hall was emitted.

Besides the ground floor guard room, two of the small rooms would be solars or private chambers for the more privileged ladies and the fourth room would serve as the castle chapel.

Lavone Andrews was consoled to find that although stripped of their finished surfaces, the floors above the vaulted ceilings of two large and two small rooms were usable. But all other floors were missing.

Only parts of the stone surrounds of the window openings were still in place. Those remnants were sketched and measured so that they could be authentically replicated in the restoration.

The distinction which made Knappogue Castle very different and set Lavone Andrews an architectural challenge was the different ages and therefore different building styles of the different phases of a castle.

The additions which had been wrapped around the original tower house had been made in the 17th, 18th and 19th centuries. The castle had remained in the ownership of the local McNamara lords for three hundred years but passed into new ownership in 1800.

The new Scott family owners were reputed to have spent what would have ranked as a fortune of eight thousand pounds on the restoration of the castle and the addition of the two-storey extension to the east of the tower.

The Scott family would not be masters of Knappogue for very long and in the wake of the desolation of the Famine of the mid-1840s, they too followed the McNamara family into ruin.

When Knappogue was sold to Theobald Fitzwalter Butler, 14th Baron Dunboyne of the ancient Irish title, the castle estate on February 23rd, 1855 extended to several thousand acres with magnificent trees, gardens and lawns.

The Dunboynes spent lavishly on the Clare residence, adding the extensive west wing and the courtyard structures. In 1899 Knappogue had passed into the ownership of Robert, the 16th Baron Dunboyne and when he retired from a legal career in London, he settled permanently at Knappogue and is buried with his wife in a grave at the front of the castle. Local legend says that he was buried in an upright position so that he could always look upon Knappogue.

It was the eve of war and also an unsettled time in Ireland when the 17th Baron Dunboyne inherited Knappogue in 1913. As a naval officer he was preoccupied with matters other than his castle in county Clare during World War I and over the same period the Easter Rising of 1916 had set the seeds that ignited into the War of Independence. Consequently the Dunboynes made their permanent home in England and made only sporadic visits to Knappogue. The castle and estate were ultimately sold in 1927 to the Land Commission of the Irish Free State for three thousand and five pounds.

In the intervening years Knappogue was systematically stripped. Roofs were removed not entirely for salvage purposes but also because property rates tax only applied to roofed buildings. World War II proved more damaging to Knappogue than World War I, the War of Independence and the Civil War when demand for timber tore out the floors, doors, windows and all other timbers from the castle and cleared the castle estate of its trees.

The measurements and sketches made on-site by Lavone Andrews to guide her restoration plans were backed up by a full set of pictures of every angle and aspect of the castle and its halls and chambers which were provided from the photographic unit at Brendan O'Regan's Shannon Free Airport Development Company.

Armed with these and as many books as they could find on architecture through the ages from the 15th to 19th centuries generally and whatever they could lay their hands on about Irish castles, Lavone Andrews and her husband returned to Houston to start on the working drawings.

They were back in Ireland in 1966 and returned with finished drawings which were "detailed and complete" Lavone Andrews recalled. The

Shannon Development company had found a reliable contractor who was prepared to make a firm bid on the restoration job if it was broken down into phases.

To extract the maximum benefit in terms of promotion and publicity that was the life support to Shannon's tourism innovations, the restoration of Knappogue was given heightened profile when a target was set of restoring life to Knappogue Castle exactly 500 years after its original tower rose up on the skyline in 1467.

In the second half of 1966, a 9-months deadline was set for Phase 1 to complete work on the ground floor for a mid-1967 opening of the castle to tourists. Towards that end, the restructuring included the conversion to use as a banquet hall of the chamber which had served as the picture gallery during the ownership by the Earls of Dunboyne.

There was a great deal more to get done. The main tower was to be roofed, windows and doors installed and, where necessary, walls of the later additions to the castle rebuilt as floors and windows were also restored. The faithful adherence to the genuine styles and standards of each period required under the restoration

partnership with the State only relented in the concessions to the 20th century for the installation of plumbing, heating and lighting.

Months before the first tour bus turned into the entrance avenue to Knappogue there was increased movement of people on the road and byways of the area. Because the new American owners insisted that, where possible, local labour should be employed, around a hundred stone masons, joiners, roofers, carpenters and labourers came from surrounding villages and farms. Their "magnificent job" in the words of Lavone Andrews was recognised and preserved when the name of each worker was inscribed in stone on a tablet in the castle entrance hall.

The Andrews happened to mention that back in their home country when a new roof was in place, it was the custom to fasten a small tree to the highest part of the roof and that this was a signal for the owners to give a party for the workmen. The locals suspected that the story was a work of fiction, but they were not going to miss out on a party. The first roof to be completed was the highest on the top of the tower rising to one hundred feet. The workmen weighed the pros and cons among themselves and ultimately an intrepid young worker clambered up to fasten a tree to the highest point of the roof.

The gesture of the workers to the American tradition was reciprocated by the Andrews who threw a party. And there were eight more roofs to go. Over the nine months period, nine roofs were completed, nine trees marked each completion and nine parties raised the proverbial roof.

On schedule and under budget, Phase 1 of the Knappogue restoration was completed and in July 1967 the keys of the castle were handed over by Mark Edwin Andrews to the then Minister for Transport and Power, Erskine Childers. The Cabinet Minister, who would be elected Ireland's third President in the following decade, was given the place of honour as lord of Knappogue for the first of the medieval banquets that would bring over one million visitors to Knappogue in the following 15 years. President Childers died during his first term in office and in bringing new vigour and visibility among the public to the presidency, his widespread engagements across the country included a visit to Knappogue. President and Mrs. Rita Childers were overnight guests at the castle. Thereafter the room where they were entertained by Mr.

and Mrs. Andrews became known as "the President's Sitting Room" and the bedroom as "the President's Bedroom". On a very low key private holiday in Ireland after his retirement, the former President of France, General Charles de Gaulle, also visited Knappogue where he had lunch and was entertained.

Phase II of the restoration included the development of two large rooms in the tower and a secondary stone stairway rising up through the balcony of a second level room to the great hall. Brought up to a standard of comfort that allowed the Andrews family to move in was the apartment in the two-storey "wraparound" addition to the original tower. In Phase II, the family quarters were finished and a chapel was installed in the old castle once again.

The chapel had not been finished when the Andrews received word that a longtime friend, the Right Reverend Henry Hobson, retired Bishop of Ohio, was arriving for a three day visit. Mr. Andrews decided to ask the bishop to consecrate the chapel. This triggered a flurry of frantic activity to select furnishings for the unfinished chapel. Mr. and Mrs. Andrews chose a 15th century iron cross that they had acquired from the steeple of a church in France, a 15th century carving of St. Erasmus, a 16th century linen-fold "monk's bench" and an unusual oak splay-fronted cupboard. But the floor of the chapel was only of rough boards and contributed to a decidedly unfinished look.

Having had a carpet for their castle quarters made in Oughterard in county Galway, the Andrews turned to the V'Soske-Joyce firm again for deliverance only to be reminded by Mrs. Joyce that they only made rugs to order. But then Mrs. Joyce remembered that a rug made to the orders of clients in Milan had never been collected. When she began to describe the rug over the phone, Lavone Andrews announced that they would head to Oughterard straight away to view the rug. They did and the rug returned with them to Knappogue. "If we had a rug designed for the room we could not have done as well," Mrs. Andrews recorded. The rug had black border bands which were the width of the arms of the black steeple cross and also had a "fleur de lis" motif matching that of the French iron cross. The colours of the rug were also just right – an ecclesiastical red blended with the colour of the castle stone. They made a point of showing this "small miracle" to Bishop Hobson when he consecrated the chapel and named it St. Mark's Chapel. The following week a joint service of blessing was held in the chapel by a Church of Ireland rector and a Roman Catholic priest. Services of all three churches were subsequently held in the chapel using the same communion vessels.

The conjunction of chance and coincidence also came into play in the decoration of a ground floor drawing room which created a connection that reached back more than a century. Adjoining what they called "the State dining room" where the former President de Gaulle dined, the Andrews had furnished the drawing room with 18th and 19th century period pieces and felt that a proper plastered ceiling would be the ideal finishing touch.

Some period houses were being torn down in Dublin at the time and salvaged from the demolition were countless pieces of the period plaster ceilings. It transpired that one of the houses had belonged to the earls of Dunboyne who had owned Knappogue in the 19th century so that part of what had been their town house was given a new lease of life in their former country castle property.

Mrs. Andrews tracked down a pair of Dublin brothers who had made the art of ceiling restoration their speciality. The pieces from the

Dublin houses were brought in plastic bags to Knappogue. On specially made boards that were to be fastened to the ceiling, the jig-saw-like pieces of ceiling plaster work were matched and assembled. Where matches for moulded pieces proved inadequate, the brothers used the pieces on hand to make rubber moulds and poured liquid plaster into the moulds to replicate the original pieces. While the work was painstaking and lengthy, it was more than worthwhile and in the view of Lavone Andrews "was much more effective than new copies could possibly have been".

Phase IV of the restoration converted the old stables to use as a craft shop and tea rooms located across a courtyard onto which the banquet guests exited from the castle. In the original order of things this was to be the final phase of the restoration, but work went on indefinitely on the buildings and the castle grounds. More than 20 years after they had brought Knappogue back to life, the Andrews were elaborating on their handiwork and added some rooms at the rear of the castle which duplicated 17th century design in a half-timbered construction.

The work of Lavone Andrews was recognised when the restoration of Knappogue Castle received an award for architectural excellence from the national heritage and preservation body, An Taisce. International recognition followed with a Europa Nostra award for restoration of a European monument. Mrs. Andrews was also accorded the rare distinction for an American woman of being admitted to membership of the Royal Institute of Architects of Ireland and was made a Fellow of the Institute when she completed 25 years of membership.

Under the original agreement worked out with Brendan O'Regan, the Andrews family made the private apartments at Knappogue their Irish residence while the ground floor area including the banquet hall was given over to the re-enacted medieval feasts and entertainment. In the glow of the publicity blitz across North America which had made the original Bunratty Castle banquet a start or finish "must" for coach tour groups, Knappogue staged two banquets per night in the April to September period and during the peak popularity of the banquets the castle regularly staged up to five banquets in a day, with daytime functions and extra night-time groups accommodated in a second smaller hall of the castle.

Knappogue also figured as one of the first day visitor attractions in Ireland and helped set the standard which brought visitor attractions around the country to more than 200 by the year 2000.

As a medieval banqueting venue and as a day visitor attraction Knappogue Castle was managed by a partnership involving two of the State agencies involved in Shannon Airport promotion. Under the banner of Castle Tours, Knappogue was managed by Flan Gleeson who had come through the hotel and hospitality sector. The Andrews family established an exceptional bond with Flan Gleeson and also with Paddy O'Grady who became the linchpin of the castle staff. The regard in which the Andrews family held Knappogue and the people who served there was manifest when Flan Gleeson and Paddy O'Grady were included among the eight pallbearers at the funeral service for Mark Edwin Andrews in 1992. In 1996 the Andrews family sold Knappogue Castle the Shannon Development agency which operated the castle entertainment and visitor centres through its Shannon Banquets and Heritage subsidiary. When Mrs. Lavone Dickensheets Andrews passed away in June of 2002, Flan Gleeson was again among the pallbearers.

The link between the Andrews family and Knappogue Castle was extended worldwide and the spirit of Knappogue preserved in an eponymous Irish whiskey.

Mark Edwin Andrews was a great fan of Irish whiskey. While establishing an Irish home at Knappogue Castle, he also began accumulating casks of Irish whiskey. By great good fortune, he managed to purchase the remaining casks of pure pot still whiskey produced at the B. Daly Distillery in Tullamore in county Offaly. The B. Daly Distillery had been established in 1829 and was the home of the famous Tullamore Dew brand. The distillery had ceased operations in 1954.

Mark Edwin stored the whiskey casks at Cork Bonded Warehouse where they continued the aging process. He and his whiskey expert would periodically test the whiskey and when they agreed that the whiskey had reached its peak, it would be bottled. He named his whiskey Knappogue Castle. The last of the whiskey, Knappogue Castle 1951, which was aged for 36 years in sherry casks, ranked as the oldest and rarest Irish whiskey in the world.

Following in his father's footsteps, Mark Andrews developed a vintage-dated Irish single malt whiskey which he named in honour of his parents' famous castle. His company, Castle Brands, owns and represents several Irish spirits brands in addition to Knappogue Castle Whiskey including Clontarf Irish whiskey, Boru Vodka, Celtic Crossing Liqueur and Brady's Irish Cream.

When Mark Edwin Andrews came to Ireland to follow a boyhood dream, the fates conspired to make reality of the fantasy. He came in search of a castle that would serve as a family residence in Ireland, so what he had in mind was not a roofless and partly derelict pile that was providing shelter for livestock. Yet destiny had dictated that his wife would be an eminent architect and that they would be brought into the orbit of Brendan O'Regan at the very time that he was conjuring a new tourism industry from the ruins of Ireland's past. In their coming together they brought an ancient McNamara castle back to life and in the process spearheaded the campaign that brought Americans flying to Ireland in droves and put in the groundwork for a tourism industry that would flourish and turn the economic tide for the west of Ireland. It was entirely appropriate that the Andrews family, having made what amounted to a monumental contribution to the shaping of the new Ireland brought something of Ireland back to the United States and that in those warmest of Irish spirits – the "uisce beatha" or water of life - a bond was established which would endure as long as Knappogue Castle.

Barbara Walters: *Uneasy introduction to Mother Ireland*

"Jeez, what a freezing country!"

That instant judgement as she stepped off the Shannon Airport airbridge on a chill October morning in 1973 introduced Ireland to Barbara Walters, the first lady of American television who within three years would also become the first million dollars a year broadcaster when she switched networks.

Ireland had been waiting for Barbara Walters but wasn't quite ready for her.

She had come with the "Today Show", the 2-hour live programme that was broadcast coast to coast five mornings a week. It was still the era of the mighty networks so that the enormous reach of "Today" and its counterparts on rival networks endowed the shows and their screen personalities with unrivalled power and influence.

Ireland had pulled off a public relations coup to take the breath away of other nations by convincing the NBC network to send its flagship show to Ireland and to transmit five shows in a row from different locations in the Republic in a sequence of all-Irish shows with the exception of breakaways back to New York for the regular daily news bulletins and updates. What seemed the unattainable daydream of bringing "Today" to Ireland had been worked on assiduously on each side of the Atlantic by the special task force of key public relations specialists drawn from the Irish public service who had been given a mandate to counter or at least moderate the devastating effects of the Northern Ireland troubles on the Irish economy and especially on tourism and industrial investment from the United States. The "Today" show had brought faraway countries to the breakfast tables of America by embarking on regular "remotes" which sent the programme, its presentation team and a battalion of support staff to countries that ranked high on the world news agenda. The "remote" before Ireland had come from Italy and the Vatican and included a very carefully choreographed appearance by the Pope.

More than a year of effort had gone into getting "Today" to Ireland. Under the flag of their

Publicity Co-Ordination Committee, Ireland's Department of Foreign Affairs pooled resources and budgets with State-funded commercial operations and key promotional agencies involved in tourism, industry and trade development to pave the way for the Ireland "remote". Most of all they had used their powers of persuasion to convince NBC that the network was not stepping into a political minefield and taking sides on the Northern Ireland issue in the propaganda campaign in which the Republic of Ireland was predictably playing second fiddle to the wiles and propaganda networks fashioned and polished over centuries by the British diplomacy machine.

With the promise of what amounted to saturation coverage of the Republic of Ireland as a bright new nation which had turned the economic corner in the 1960s by opening up to the overseas investment and knowhow largely coming from the United States, nobody was under any illusion regarding the critical importance of making "Today" in Ireland an unqualified success.

At every level from government to the high-level security operation that was put in place and down to the hand-picked team of limousine drivers who ferried the high profile stars and executives anonymously around the country, everyone was on their toes and every detail checked and re-checked.

The giant NBC network was also pulling out all the stops to make sure that all went smoothly. Besides having to justify the massive cost of uprooting its entire show and operating with hired-in outside broadcast units, no effort had to be spared in making sure that every need and whim of its celebrity-status presenters and executive producer were indulged.

The lengths, in the literal sense of the term, which the NBC network would go to in order to keep everyone sweet was demonstrated a few days in advance of the advent of Barbara Walters and her co-presenters.

For a number of weeks before the transmissions were to be beamed out from Ireland, the "Today" team arrived in relays. First the administration and secretarial staff who set up the co-ordination offices at Dromoland Castle Hotel in Clare; the Brandon Hotel in Tralee, county Kerry and the Gresham Hotel in Dublin. They were closely followed by researchers and writers and set designers who dispersed to the three centres to draft up outlines of the programmes to be put to the decision makers when they arrived.

Heralding that the big names would follow just a few days behind was a man whose very ordinary appearance and behaviour belied the status that he was accorded by the others of the advance party. His function was essential to the smooth running of the operation and therefore he was of highly important status.

The man knew his job and precisely what he had to do. Once he had checked in and touched base with his network colleagues, he requested admission to the suites that would be occupied by the "Today" elite. They were the executive producer, Stuart Schulberg, brother of the writer of Oscar winning "On The Waterfront" and the trio of co-presenters. The most seasoned presenter was Frank Magee who had been swept from news correspondent to national profile and prestige after anchoring the live unbroken coverage from Dallas that followed the assassination of President John F Kennedy. He was the dapper figure of charm with a soft but mature broadcasting voice. Balancing the newsman's gravitas of Magee was Joe Garigiola, a retired baseball catcher who had built an award-winning second career as a sports broadcaster and whose extrovert popular appeal brought him into the "Today" line-up. Already a mould-breaker was Barbara Walters who had become the role model for female aspirants to a career in news and current affairs television.

When she set foot in Ireland, Barbara Walters was also just a step away from a career peak unmatched by any woman in television but, thoroughly in keeping with her career path, was only to be a springboard to even higher achievement. Forty-two years old in 1973, she had relentlessly moved up the ladder since joining the writing team on the ratings topping "Today" in 1961. Within three years she had made the switch to reporter and her no-frills style of interviewing combined with her super-confident readiness to take on any assignment was the basis for her 1970 book "How to Talk to Practically Anybody About Practically Anything". Her stature in what had been a male dominated world also landed her the anchor role for the "Not For Women Only" talk show. With "Today" she became a household name and an oft-parodied voice on American television and a prize asset of NBC. The network made use of its star woman, sending her on President

Richard Nixon's history-making visit to the Peoples Republic of China in 1972.

So when Barbara Walters came to Ireland in October 1973, she was quite certain of her importance to "Today" and to the NBC network. NBC was equally aware of her value and the following year would elevate her to first woman co-host of "Today" which won her an Emmy in her first year in the job. That milestone most probably catapulted her to the highest heights when she was lured away in 1976 with the television first of a million dollars a year deal and become the first woman to co-host the CBS evening news alongside one of the luminaries of news broadcasting, Harry Reasoner.

It was understandable then that when "Today" came to Ireland that the top brass at NBC were very much pre-occupied with keeping their star broadcaster happy. It was to make absolutely and completely sure that all three of the co-presenters got identical treatment that the advance man did a sweep of the three suites at Dromoland Castle Hotel to be occupied by Walters, Magee and Garagiola. It was not a sweep for bugging or other surveillance devices. The man from NBC was using a measuring tape. He measured every dimension of the three suites, including the drapes and fittings, the furnishings and the windows. When the measurements were completed, he was satisfied that not one of the co-presenters occupied a suite that was a fraction of an inch larger or smaller than any of the other two suites. His next task was to make sure that the castle stocked the liquor of choice of the "Today" elite. When it was discovered that some of the favourite brands were not available, arrangements were made to access the bonded stores of the Shannon Duty Free Store so that liquors otherwise sold only as exported tax-free buys could be added to the drinks cabinets at Dromoland. With instructions that fresh buckets of ice were to be in the suites at all times, the advance scout from NBC could then move on to make identical checks at the hotel nerve-centres in Tralee in the south west and then in the Dublin capital.

It was with such painstaking detail that everything possible had been prepared in advance for the "Today Show" in Ireland to get into full swing. All things and all the people involved were in readiness. All except the suite for Ms. Barbara Walters.

The three top of the range hotels picked out as the co-ordination bases for the 5 "Today" transmissions were on a special deal. In return for laying on the accommodation and hospitality, the quid-pro-quo arrangement meant that the hotels got "commercial message" slots that would normally have been not only outside the range of their budgets but also shut out by the demand for the premium slots during the run of the "Today" show.

First base for "Today" was Dromoland Castle, the castle and estate of the ancient O'Brien clan which gave the first touch of luxury for a fledgling Irish tourism industry when it was bought and refurbished by the Irish-American industrialist, Bernard McDonough.

Dromoland and the new generation of hotels that had followed in its wake in the economic resurrection of the west of Ireland from the 1960s, were geared to the American market and, as the first stop on the north Atlantic run into Europe, special conditions prevailed around the Shannon Airport gateway.

Transatlantic flights touched down at Shannon in the early morning hours and were often an hour or more ahead of schedule having being helped across the ocean by tailwinds. Even though they had travelled by night and could grab a few hours sleep on the way, passengers arrived in Ireland bleary eyed and weary and ready for bed. Consequently the hotels and other accommodations that served the North American market needed to have bedrooms vacant and ready by early morning. In most cases this meant that the room was either kept vacant from the previous night or that guests gave a guarantee to vacate the room in the dawn hours.

Nothing was being left to chance with "Today" arrangements so that contingency provisions were built into each element of the operational plan and, in the case of the hotel accommodation, reservations for each "Today" individual were made to start a day ahead of their actual day of arrival – just to make absolutely sure that the room would be available as soon as the guest arrived.

It was some time into the build-up of "Today" personnel in Ireland that the Dromoland Castle general manager, Ms. Patricia Barry cottoned on to the fact that her castle suites and rooms were being held vacant and not bringing in any revenues for her hotel in the interests of keeping everybody at "Today" happy.

Like Barbara Walters, but in a different field and in a different country, Patricia Barry was also a trail-blazer for professional women who were an extremely rare species in an Ireland where women had to retire from State employment when they married. She was a member of the prominent business and political family whose tea importing and blending business in the city of Cork was a national leader. She was one of the talented and dynamic women whose gifts had been recognised by Brendan O'Regan at his Shannon Airport catering and sales empire. Remarkably for the Ireland of the time, she had been sent to the USA to spearhead promotion of Ireland and Shannon alongside Bill Maxwell who would become the publicity director first in the USA and finally at Dublin headquarters for the Irish national airline, Aer Lingus.

Patricia Barry had been hired by the Dromoland millionaire Bernard McDonough and ran the castle with a will of steel. Not a woman to be awed by fortunes or status, when "Today" came to Dromoland in 1973 her brother Peter had earlier that year received from the President of Ireland his seal of office as Minister for Transport and Power in the ruling coalition government in which his Fine Gael party was joined by a Labour Party junior partner.

On the evening before Barbara Walters arrived, Ms. Barry made a call to the "Today" co-ordination office located in an annex of the hotel.

"Is Ms. Walters arriving in the morning?" she enquired.

"Yes, Ms. Barry".

"It is certain that she is arriving?"

"Why Ms. Barry, is there a problem?"

"Well yes. I've sold the room and it's occupied tonight". She anticipated the next question when adding –"and I cannot move the guests out before morning".

"How early can you have them out of the room Ms. Barry?"

"We shall do our best to make it as early as possible. When do you expect Ms. Walters?"

"We have had tailwinds all week and the Met people say that there is no reason to expect any change, so she could be on the ground as early as 6 o'clock in the morning".

Barbara Walters and the "Today" elite were not going to have to wait around at the Shannon terminal to collect their bags. That had all been taken care of as part of the special arrangements being laid on at every juncture where there was even the slightest chance of a hiccup.

"Can you slow things down at the airport to delay her arrival here?"

"We'll see what can be arranged Ms. Barry".

"Do your best," Patricia Barry urged.

A stall the stars exercise to buy time for Dromoland was drawn up. The fabled capacity of Shannon Airport to effortlessly respond to any exigency was activated. Seasoned catering staff whose capacity to respond to the irregular comings and goings of 1950s transatlantic flights was the keystone in building the airport's reputation and putting Ireland on the world aviation map, were summoned in early to stage a welcoming reception for the "Today" arrivals. In recognition of the special status of the guests, they were to be treated in the VIP lounge with the airport's speciality Irish Coffee brew. All handled as if coffee laced with Irish whiskey and smoothened for consumption by fresh natural cream was something normal before 7 o'clock in the morning.

An outsize bouquet of flowers for presentation to Ms. Walters was ordered. And on the strength of favours owed and promised, a couple of the local newspaper stringers were prevailed on to make an early rise and appearance to interview the US network celebrities.

With those arrangements in place, the Irish side of the "Today" co-ordination team went to bed with a prayer that the tailwinds on the north Atlantic would abate.

Barbara Walters stepped regally into Ireland to be met by a greeting party, the scent of flowers, the aroma of Irish Coffee and the curiosity of a couple of news reporters. She was having none of it. Swathed to her chin in fur and exuding the finely tuned alertness of a highly-strung thoroughbred, Barbara Walters and Ireland in October did not hit it off. Whatever lay ahead, just then she had just one thing in mind – to get to her limousine and then to her hotel with the utmost speed.

A quick call was made from the Shannon terminal building to Dromoland. The message was short but ominous. "Ms. Walters is on her way". Nobody was in any hurry to get a ringside seat at the castle. There Ms. Walters seethed and strode up and down the reception hall in impatient fury. Waiting for Ms. Barry. Waiting for an apology. Waiting for an explanation. When those two formidable ladies did meet up, nobody was witness to what transpired and nobody enquired. Only Ms. Barbara Walters and Ms. Patricia Barry know precisely what happened when their worlds collided.

Once they had rested in their suites and with everyone from the hand-picked drivers of the CIE limousine fleet to the special co-ordination teams set up by the Irish State agencies and the hotel staff dancing attendance on them, the "Today" elite woke up to a more appealing Ireland then the first impressions through bleary eyes at their early morning landing. But, even with the Dromoland Castle heating system replicating American standard comfort, they were still feeling the cold. They mentioned "thermal clothing" and most of a day was spent checking around with suppliers from top department stores to winter sports outfitters before the penny dropped that what they meant was the "long johns" or combinations underwear of the grandfather generations in Ireland.

With a day or two to spare before going on air, they took advantage of their chauffeured limousines for a little touring, taking in the natives oblivious to their celebrity status as well as the scenes and sights. They also did some shopping. Naturally, Barbara Walters had a different way of shopping. Because the first Duty Free Store in the world at Shannon was to feature in the opening show, she had picked up that once visitors could flash their return tickets they could do their duty free shopping in advance and either arrange to pick it up when departing from Shannon or have their buys mailed back to the States.

In a matter of days she made a couple of excursions to the Shannon Duty Free which in 1974 was the largest of its kind in the world. And while she may have picked up a favourite perfume at the tax-free cost, it was not the prestige brands that brought out her credit card. She went for the native Irish products. Tweed and linen and most of all the hand-knit Aran wear. She was so taken with the sweaters, cardigans and tasseled hats and caps that she bought in bulk with her daughter Jacqueline particularly in mind. Her enthusiasm for the Aran knits was so infectious that it was decided to fit out the three co-presenters in Aran knits as part of their on-screen wardrobes.

Even as she climbed the broadcasting ladder from her college days writing press releases for her local radio station, Barbara Walters was no stranger to celebrity. Although she was born in Boston, she grew up surrounded by celebrities because her father owned "The Latin Quarter" night club frequented by the stars. The celebrity status of others made no impression on Barbara Walters and showed in her interviewing style. But in the year that she had made it to the top tier at "Today" when becoming one of the co-presenters and first woman in that role, she was very aware of her own celebrity and that showed during her shopping trip to the Shannon Duty Free Store.

Predictably the Americans picking up duty-free booze, cigars and cigarettes and gifts while waiting to board their flights recognised the face that visited most homes across the US every morning. They tried to give the impression that they too were just browsing through the aisles showcasing Ireland's and Europe's finest merchandise. But they hovered and circled as Barbara Walters walked among them. With an escort minder discreetly signaling to shoppers not to approach, they kept their distance. All except for one rash shopper who decided to go for it. She was a mature American lady. As she moved forward, she said – "Barbara, you don't know me from Adam…"

Without looking up from the merchandise she was perusing, Barbara Walters snapped back –"that's right" as she turned and walked away.

But there was no sign of the prickly Barbara Walters when she simply became part of the crowd and came face to face with Ireland old and new at the medieval banquet at 15th century Bunratty Castle and then crossed the road and five centuries to join contemporary boisterous revelry at Durty Nelly's old world pub.

It was part bonding exercise and part release valve for the strains and tensions of mounting a mammoth live television undertaking in entirely unfamiliar surroundings that brought the "Today" to the castle banquet where the finely tuned balance of rowdy merry making with the finest of Irish traditional song and music was an enchantment. The secret ingredient of the castle banquets does not feature on the menu. The absence of cutlery is the great leveller. Supping broth direct from the bowl, breaking up cakes of bread into individual shares, gnawing on spare ribs from the hand and tackling a chicken with only a knife blows away all the niceties of convention and dining protocols. Feasting shoulder to shoulder at long tables while mead and red wine splashes out generously into goblets sweeps away all distinctions of class, creed or nationality. Everyone is equal at a medieval banquet, so nobody paid the least bit of attention to the television personalities among them.

Sensibly the "Today" team and crew were bussed to the first sitting of the twice-nightly castle feasts which provided the scope for an alcohol sign-off to the night at "Durty Nelly's". What lay ahead at Bunratty had not initially appealed to Barbara Walters. She was inclined to cry off. Eventually she was persuaded to sample the castle banquet at least and her limousine was on stand by to whisk her from one castle to another at any time of her choosing. She stayed to the end of the Bunratty meal and entertainment and by then she was ready for more. So Barbara Walters joined the flow across the road to the "Durty Nelly's" warren of crowded intimate bars and was one of the crowd as, glass in hand and standing on the window seat in the piano bar, she joined with other forty-somethings in the company of natives and tourists as they belted out evergreens and popular hits of the early 70s.

The first day of "Today" in Ireland came from Shannon Airport with a wistful ballad evocation of Irish exile, "Steer My Bargue to Erin's Isle" accompanying the opening shots of an Aer Lingus jumbo easing its way in over the new Ireland of overseas industry and new multi-nation town that had grown up around Shannon since the 1960s. Frank Magee introduced the week-long series from the roof of the tallest office block in Shannon where a garden studio of fresh greenery had been assembled overnight by the NBC set designers. Day one went smoothly, but there was a nagging undercurrent of anxiety that Ms. Walters was not entirely relaxed.

Day two came from Bunratty Castle and its surrounding Folk Park depicting 19th century Irish life. And while Barbara Walters was still unsettled, she was charmed by the old world cottages and the traditional crafts perpetuated in the park. The authentically restored and re-furnished castle was the centrepiece of the broadcast, with songs from the castle entertainers and interviews at the blacksmith's forge and the workshop of the blind basket weaver blended with a featurette on three American writers who had made their homes in Ireland. Throughout Ms. Walters was being sensitively chaperoned by the most senior figures from NBC and the Irish co-coordinating hosts. The day's punishing schedule was only a prelude. Later in the day would come the transfer to the 75 miles distant location for the third and fourth programmes. Barbara Walters was not looking forward to the journey or the pressures involved in preparing for the next day's programme from the Tralee capital of county Kerry. Her thoughts were back in New York. "You know John, my daughter would simply love it here," she told her escort as they strolled in the rustic quiet of the folk park. That comment hatched an idea from John Dilger, publicity manager at the Shannon Free Airport Development Company and national co-ordinator for "Today" in Ireland.

Even as the "Today" show departed the Shannon area and headed south, moves were afoot to make Ireland a little more like home for Barbara Walters. John Dilger too was on the move with the television caravan and retinue. But he left instructions on what was to be done.

What had to be done had to be done quickly and secretly and also in a matter of hours because of the time difference between New York and Ireland which meant that calls to set up arrangements could not really get moving until the early afternoon at the earliest in Ireland. The New York office of the Aer Lingus airline took care of the transport arrangements when setting aside a couple of seats in the first class section of that evening's jumbo flight out of Kennedy. The airline also arranged for a limousine to pick up the two passengers.

Courtesy of the top brass from NBC who traveled with the "Today" party, the co-coordinating office at the Shannon base had been provided with details of where Barbara Walters lived and her ex-directory phone number.

A call was made to the New York apartment of Ms. Walters where her adopted daughter Jacqueline was being looked after by her French governess. The governess was referred to as "mademoiselle" but more familiarly as "Zelle".

The governess seemed not the least surprised by the call from Ireland and the instructions that she and Jacqueline were to pack their bags and be ready that evening to be picked up by limousine and taken to their flight to Shannon.

Then came the bombshell. "I don't have a passport," the governess confessed.

She was told not to worry and to proceed as instructed.

From Shannon calls were made to the French Embassy, the situation explained and the name of the governess passed on so that arrangements could be made to issue her with an emergency passport once she was in Ireland.

The importance of the "Today" show in Ireland and the arrangements which were being made to bring the daughter of Ms. Walters to join her on location were also understood by the Irish emigration and customs people at Shannon.

Special arrangements were made to have a special desk in place where "Zelle" and her young charge could complete the formalities out of sight of the prying eyes of the other passengers.

From New York came confirmation that the child and her governess had been picked up, delivered to Kennedy and were actually in the air and on their way to Ireland.

With tail winds again favouring fuel-saving and early landing, the Aer Lingus 747 touched down at Shannon not long after 6 o'clock in the morning.

Greeters were standing by at the mouth of the airbridge and just a few strides away was the special desk put in place overnight where two senior officials were waiting to process the French governess and the celebrity broadcaster's daughter.

The governess stepped off first and held up a hand. "I found my passport", she gushed.

"Put it away" her greeters hissed to spare the embarrassment of telling the officials that they had been dragged from their beds for no reason.

Less than two hours later, Jacqueline and her governess walked into the Brandon Hotel in the town of Tralee where the second "Today" co-ordinating centre had been up and running for a couple of weeks as researchers and writers put the programme together. Overnight Barbara Walters had been taking in the background and other details of the personalities lined up for interview. The third show from Ireland was taking up the theme of the Irish horse breeding industry. While soaking up the colour and vitality of a race meeting in rural Ireland, the programme was to feature the Irish-American industrialist and bloodstock owner, John A Mulcahy who had also endowed Irish tourism with two luxury hotels. Complementing the self-made man who had brought Pfizer Corporation investment to Ireland was the prolific Irish playwright, bar keeper, wit and teller of tall tales, John B Keane.

But the stresses and strains of bringing "Today" to Ireland evaporated when Jacqueline ran into the arms of her mother. The bigwigs of NBC could only look on in awesome recognition that John Dilger was much more than a debonair charmer while "J.D." to his intimates permitted himself a satisfied smile as he basked in the acclamation as an unrivalled fixer. The unease and strains that had permeated the set and the fringes of "Today" in Ireland were banished never to return in the later programmes from Dublin showcasing Irish culture and heritage and opening up a coast to coast American audience for a government Minister to deliver the government line on Ireland's unchanging attractions for tourists, industry and investment.

Back in Shannon later that day a call came in from New York. Not to get confirmation that all had gone smoothly on Irish soil but to mention a detail that had been overlooked.

"You realise that we have just abducted the adopted daughter of Barbara Walters," was the confession that suggested that there had been unwitting collaboration on the Irish side also.

It was hastily explained that Barbara Walters was separated from her second husband and that taking the child out of the jurisdiction without telling anyone (including Barbara Walters) could cause an almighty hullabaloo.

But that story was one that stayed untold.

Chuck Feeney: *Super salesman behind University's rise*

It took more than 130 years for the city of Limerick to catch up on sister cities in third level education but just one American to put its new university ahead of the field.

It was only a matter of time before the University of Limerick and Charles "Chuck" Feeney were brought together. After all they had so much in common.

The archives of "The Limerick Chronicle", the 1768-founded oldest newspaper in the Republic of Ireland, record the return with almost clockwork regularity of the local debate that centred on the issue of a university for Ireland's third city. Election candidates fumed at the indignity suffered by the city when Galway got its university alongside Dublin and Cork. Elected representatives at all levels were guaranteed a hearing and media coverage when demanding university status for the city. Most insistently, in a trading city of merchants who distinguished themselves in civic leadership, the business community refused to leave the university question unanswered. Limerick Chamber of Commerce, which spearheaded or was in the vanguard of milestone initiatives that raised the prestige and profile of the city, aired the university slight at every opportunity and launched or joined regular campaigns demanding university status for the city.

Yet for more than a century the campaigns, pleas and lobbying were no more than a recurring irritant for government decision makers. But then Shannon Airport opened up a new era of communication and a new high-tempo flow of new ideas and new people which combined to bring 20th century thinking as well as technologies and knowhow to the region around the airport. The cause of a university for Limerick was taken up with renewed vigour. But this time around it picked up compelling momentum because getting a university was no longer seen as a sore point of injured city pride. This time it was about building a future for the most venerable of Irish cities tracing its roots back to Viking settlers and with a City Charter of 1197 from King John that was older than London's.

Shannon Airport had come from nowhere in 1945 and fifteen years later had conjured up an industrial revolution from nowhere. On reclaimed mudflats in a remote corner of Europe, Shannon was starting point to a turning point in Ireland's economic history. The natural hospitality which was the hallmark of Irishness was given new dimensions. Through the air gateway of Shannon Airport, Ireland was extending open arms not only to the well-heeled dollar-dispensing American tourist and was also opening a door to Europe for foreign industry. So that the vulnerable balance of the still insular and tariff-protected Irish economy would not be upset, implanting of overseas industry was kept under control and restricted to export only activity within the duty-free and tax free enclave around Shannon Airport. When put before top Irish business figures, the idea was laughed to derision. But multinational corporations had different ideas. General Electric came to Shannon. So too did the great diamond-based conglomerate De Beers corporation of South Africa whose scouting team for a first base in Europe had chosen Shannon for a pioneering partnership. Where General Electric and De Beers went, others followed. With the first State training centre for industrial skills as support, the new generation of new name industries

clustering around Shannon Airport rapidly became the training ground for a generation of Irish workers many of whom had returned from far-flung foreign climes. Just as work experience in the Shannon Airport kitchens had become an international visa for chefs and catering staff and later for graduates of the spin-off hotel management school, the inflow of modern technologies and techniques, coupled with Irish aptitude and eagerness to learn and earn, made the pool of English-speaking employees at Shannon a major asset in attracting even more investment. Bringing with them a culture of recognising and cultivating talent, the early arrivals at the new Shannon Industrial Estate showpiece created a reservoir of skilled labour and the new firms functioned as a management academy. The spectacular trail blazing success of the Shannon industrial initiative was extended to the entire country with transforming impact through the 1960s. The trail through Shannon was followed by new American industries which, with the availability of experienced recruits poached from Shannon, brought new sophisticated products and skills to the region around Shannon. The ripple effect from Shannon made the city of Limerick a prime location for the new investment that flowed across the Atlantic from the mid-60s. As a bright new dawn opened up, the transformation was accompanied by the call for a university. This time the influential voices of the new overseas firms spoke up for the city and made the telling point that essential on-going development and performance of the new industries and their export products would rely heavily on an educated workforce. Graduates were going to be in demand. Besides its teacher training college, Limerick did not boast a third level education institution and consequently could not provide a ready supply of graduates. This time round the bureaucrats listened to Limerick's claim to a university. It helped mightily that a dynamic and change-driving Minister for Education whose premature death would be a numbing loss, was the charismatic Donogh O'Malley, who represented the constituency centred on Limerick city.

The fusion of local leadership with the powerful new leverage provided by overseas industry spilling over into Limerick that ultimately delivered third level education to the city was promoted from Shannon. Paul Quigley, the ex Irish Army officer who was the first Director of the Irish Management Institute before being he was head-hunted to become the first General Manager at the Shannon Free Airport Development Company, chaired the group which spearheaded the final campaign for a university for Limerick. But when Limerick finally got a third level educational, it was not quite a university.

What Limerick got was something completely new and therefore different. That it was different was emphasised by the established universities whose academics regarded the fledgling Limerick effort as an upstart with delusional ideas about its status. But being different and new was turned to Limerick's advantage through the appointment of Edward Walsh as the first Director of what was initially the Limerick Institute of Higher Education. He was from Cork but came to Limerick from the United States bringing with him a new outlook and vision very much based on what he had seen in North America. What he wished to shape was on the lines of the Massachusetts Institute of Technology, a buzzing rather than a sedate seat of modern learning and innovative thinking geared to technology and enterprise that would cultivate intelligence as a resource in turning out new crops of graduates.

Although they tried, entrenched interests could not stop what was seen as the new Limerick pretender. The very fact that it was all new and different provided Ed Walsh and the closely-knit team he gathered around him with not simply a wide canvas but with virtually unlimited possibilities. With self-imposed limitations the only restraint on imagination and vision, the mission that started from the elegant "White House" manor residence on the Plassey estate on the fringe of Limerick city, established the second engine of growth which with Shannon Airport lifted an entire region to heights that would win 1970s recognition and plaudits from the OECD (Organisation of Economic Co-Operation and Development) and the European Parliament.

The bright new arrival on the academic scene with the bright new ideas about linkage between higher education and the emerging industrial and business sectors got much the same treatment as that reception given over a decade earlier to the concept of an industrial zone around Shannon Airport. Skeptics and doubters abounded who regarded the new presence in Limerick as an upstart with an exaggerated sense of its own importance that needed to be put in its place. The resentment of the establishment within the halls of academe and the corridors of bureaucratic rule made itself plainly felt. Programmes of study were ridiculed; the credentials of lecturing staff as well as accreditation and the status of qualifications to be gained at Limerick were questioned and obstructed. The view from the other city seats of learning in the country was played out at the official opening of the new Limerick institute when 600 guests attended a black tie dinner celebration. The blatant affront from tables of academic guests representing the universities who carried on with boisterous chatter throughout the formal speeches on Limerick's big occasion only served to steel the determination of Edward Walsh and Limerick to make a go of their third level college.

From the outset the new college had an ally in Shannon Development and the closest of close relationships extended to overlap at the highest levels of the two organisations with Ed Walsh serving as a member of the Board of Directors at the regional development agency and top Shannon Development figures appointed to seats including the chair of the college's Governing Body. At practical levels, the two organisations responded to the immediate and planning requirements of economic development in the region around Limerick with joint initiatives. A Regional Management Centre for advancement of training and development brought senior figures from the region's growing manufacturing sector into direct decision-making involvement. The partnership approach between the college, the State promotion agency and the manufacturing-business sector continued with the establishment of the country's first Innovation Centre. Based on the college campus, the centre laid on modern but low cost facilities in shared services and with access to the guidance and inputs of the enterprise agency and the college to create an incubator unit in which new enterprises could be helped to get on their feet before venturing out into the chill climate of uncompromising international competition.

But whatever the new thinking and new initiatives that sprang from the old world Plassey estate watered by the Shannon where the third level college was putting down its roots, its very newness rankled with the academic establishment. Limerick was the brash newcomer. Limerick was delusional and harboured ambitions above its station in the academic order of things. Limerick was all big ideas and big talk. Limerick was an upstart.

Limerick's aspiring university was long on vision and short on funds. It was also the new breed of underdog that was yapping and snapping at the heels that shot out sharp repelling kicks from under gowns of venerable academic office.

Limerick and its wannabe university were just the right fit for Chuck Feeney. He was an American billionaire from working class beginnings who had brought astonishing and transforming new meaning to the term "secret admirer"... He had decided to bring good fortune to hand-picked causes but the good fortune he brought was of a profoundly covert nature. Through the Atlantic Foundation that Feeney set up in 1987 to manage his philanthropy there was no give-away about his give-aways. Appeals, petitions and pleas did not work. Nondescript almost to the nonentity invisibility which he favoured, Chuck Feeney not only personally picked out the good causes that matched up to his judgement of worthwhile efforts, he also personally checked them out and did so in such a subtle fashion that even the recipients of funding that was most often beyond their wildest dreams would only suspect that the nice but very retiring Mr. Feeney had something to do with it.

The new Limerick arrival on Ireland's higher education scene had many attractive features for

Feeney. It's very newness and breezy self-confidence that unsettled the establishment smacked more of American campus life than the hallowed halls of the National University of Ireland seats of learning at Dublin, Cork and Galway which looked down from exalted seniority dating back to the first half of the 19th century. The vision projected by Ed Walsh reflected the North American academic background that he had been forsaken to take up what could well have been a Limerick poisoned chalice. Instead of fitting in with the established universities, he virtually imposed himself and his Limerick brand as a force for change on the entire education system. Very much on the lines of the Massachusetts Institution of Technology, the core concept was for a contemporary university that would reflect and project the robust vigour and youth of a modern Ireland that saw itself in the context of the new Europe. A world of change was emerging from technology and innovation.

Just as Shannon Airport had proven fertile ground for planting the first seeds of overseas industry, knowhow and export performance, the new third level institute at Limerick was geared and eager to work with private enterprise and not at the different sides of the fence which elsewhere separated the higher planes of the academic world from the ground level realities of commercial and business life. The Limerick college wanted to share its campus and its thinking power with a mix of mature overseas ventures and fledgling Irish enterprises and tap the energy generated to establish an intelligence reservoir from which a hotbed of activity and an incubation centre could be fuelled.

Like Brendan O'Regan at Shannon, Chuck Feeney and Ed Walsh were men who saw the big picture. When Feeney cast a searching eye over the Ireland of his ancestors, he saw modernisation of higher education as the key to the 21st century Ireland that was coming up fast. In Limerick he found leaders who talked his language and like him they were also doers.

There was yet another irresistible force that brought Chuck Feeney and the University of Limerick together. At surface level it was Duty Free shopping. But deeper down it was the power of trading and doing business together to bring about understanding and the organised harmony that common cause and mutual benefits builds among peoples. And at the root were an instinctive empathy with people and a genuine passion for delivering service to a standard of quality worthy of the person being served.

Duty Free was the magic formula that bonded Elmore, New Jersey-born Chuck Feeney with Shannon Airport in the land of his forefathers. The "free of duty" concept was as old as shipping movements through the great ports. Ports like Danzig were promoted as "freeports" and gained an edge on competitors with concessions to shipping on the duties to be levied. Shannon Airport attempted to graft the concept onto air transport in 1947. But while the proclamation of the successor to the Foynes flying boat landfall in Europe as a "Free Airport" put the new re-fuelling staging post on the world aviation map, it would take some years and a touch of America-inspired genius to originate what was to become a global phenomenon.

On the Duty Free trail Chuck Feeney followed in the slipstream of the Irish government appointed Shannon Airport supremo Brendan O'Regan. Their paths were separated by almost a decade but each led to transforming enrichment. For Shannon Airport, the Duty Free was the start of a confidence-instilling series of initiatives which would reverse more than a century of spirits-sapping decline in the west of Ireland. For Chuck Feeney Duty Free was a ticket to undreamed of riches which he converted to a round-trip when deciding to give away the billions from the personal fortune that 30 years of global leadership in Duty Free sales had won him. Although their lives were shaped on different sides of the Atlantic, for each man the American way was to point the way.

The "free airport" designation of Shannon Airport was simply that, a tag which signaled that the potential of air transport for an island nation struggling to establish an identity was recognised by the Irish who wanted to make more of it. Then the Marshall Plan changed all that.

Brendan O'Regan was selected in an elite group of four from Ireland who joined a dozen more from neighbouring European countries on a six weeks swing through the United States. War had brought the USA and Europe closer together and not just as allies. The critical importance of communication and movement of personnel and equipment in World War II had massively accelerated advance in air transport. The peacetime follow-on effects were appreciated in the United States. Transatlantic travel was shaping up to evolve into a mass movement with commercial aviation carriers bringing fares within the reach of the income groups the airlines needed to fill the vastly multiplied seat capacity. The Marshall Plan tour was set up to familiarise leaders from the old world hospitality sector of Europe with the standards and fare that were an everyday feature of life in the United States and which Americans would demand if trips to Europe were not to be a disappointment.

The world of difference that he came face to face with on that American tour made such an impact on Brendan O'Regan that he did what in most circumstances would have been seen as disloyal. The supremo who was in charge of Shannon Airport and had pinned his ambitions and plans to the tail of aviation from the war-time flying boat days at Foynes, chose to return to Ireland by ocean liner. The experience of all grades of the American hospitality industry – from the pandering peaks of service of the millionaire retreats to the spick and span utility of the budget motel, from the exclusive restaurant to the counter of the diner – gave him so much food for thought that O'Regan wanted time to digest it all. He was tasked to come back with a report. Instead he assembled an action agenda that would radically extend the life expectancy of his re-fuelling stop airport and make Shannon the logical gateway to Ireland for American travellers.

It was on that 1950 voyage home that O'Regan's eyes were opened to the full potential of duty free sales. Outside territorial waters, passengers on the "SS America" could buy liquor and tobacco products at tax-free prices. The revenue possibilities of the on-board duty free shop were not being fully tapped but were not missed by the Irishman. Back at Shannon he had a duty-free airport where legislation calculated to draw payload placed the airport zone outside the reach of government tax impositions. There was also an airport shop. But up to then what amounted to no more than a kiosk dealt largely in crafts and souvenirs. Shannon did sell liquor duty-free, but that was confined to airline crews. Now the thought dawned of combining the shop and the duty free concessions and the world's first airport Duty Free Store was conceived at sea.

For Chuck Feeney too travel did more than broaden the mind. It opened his eyes and opened the way for the modest start-up of what would become in the following 25 years the biggest retail chain in the world. His intuitive gift for identifying ways of bringing in money was evident from his boyhood. School year weekends saw him caddying on his local golf course and during the summer vacation he rented out towels and umbrellas at the Point Pleasant resort in his home state of New Jersey. The agile mind that won him a scholarship to Regis High School in Manhattan where the Jesuits shaped "young men of superior intellect and leadership potential" was also at work through his years in the military. He enlisted four months after graduation in June 1948, learned to speak the language when posted to Japan and had his service extended on the 1950 outbreak of the Korean War from which Feeney emerged with the rank of Sergeant and his name changed for the remainder of his life from Charles to "Chuck".

His flair as a salesman re-emerged when he took the opportunity under the GI Bill to attend university and chose Cornell College which was renowned in and beyond the United States as the leader in turning out top bracket executive material for the hospitality and leisure sectors. During his years there he established a niche as "the sandwich man", taking orders and delivering to his fellow under graduates and he also turned a profit selling football programmes

and made a seasonal return to schoolboy enterprise as a purveyor of Christmas cards.

When he graduated from Cornell in 1956 Feeney followed the post-war trail of thousands of fellow Americans by taking off on an extended – wherever it takes me – tour of Europe. In the south of France, it was not the opulent lifestyle of the idle rich, exiled royalty and bluebloods from another age that caught his eye. Instead it was the conspicuous presence of the US Navy in gigantic numbers of servicemen. And when he discovered that the servicemen were entitled to a quota of duty-free liquor each month, he hit the jackpot.

Within the decade his Tourists International was ranked as one of the world's first global retail operations, doing business in 27 countries. The rapid ascent had been brought about by a mix of an instinctive eye for an opening and trail blazing innovation. On the tide of liquor sales to the men of the US Sixth Fleet around the Mediterranean, the enterprise was just two years in existence and had expanded its merchandise range to perfumes, watches, cameras and the novelty of transistor radios when Tourists International took a stand at the Brussels World Fair of 1958. The full range of merchandise was brought under one roof with a trail blazing "one stop shop" in Paris and was followed by the promotional innovation of the perforated tear-off coupon.

Vast new markets were opened up by simply ferreting out what turned out to be hugely enriching sales opportunities which were tucked away in the fine print of tax regulations. A gigantic market with limitless repeat order potential was identified back home in the USA when Feeney and partners discovered that Americans in 15 US states were entitled to buy a gallon of liquor free of duty every 31 days. While copy-cat ventures joined the hooch home delivery stampede, Feeney and friends had been first into the field and made the first killings.

Overseas a major new stream of high-value business arrived on wheels. It emerged that Americans returning to the United States qualified for exemption from tax duties and levies when they bought a car and brought it back to the USA. On the strength of that concession Tourists International was selling one thousands cars per week in 1964.

But it was not one jackpot after another. The sheer pace of growth and of profit making proved almost too much to handle at one stage.

The runaway success of the duty free business threatened to run off the management rails but corrective action was taken in time to stabilise the business. In the duty free business there were always more ups than downs. The 1960s boom in Japanese tourism brought repeated the spectacular success in Europe and the USA with the opening of the first chain of Duty Free Stores in the Asia-Pacific region. By the 1980s Duty Free Shoppers was the largest retailer in the world and the biggest single retailer in Hong Kong, Hawaii, Alaska and Guam. With yearly sales of hovering around € 250million, duty free customers had made Chuck Feeney a personal fortune that placed him among the 25 richest Americans listed by the prestige "Forbes" business magazine.

By this time Chuck Feeny had started to give his money away. Initially it was simply responding to appeals. His alma mater Cornell College pitched for a contribution of one thousand dollars – he sent a cheque for ten thousand. That was in the 1960s, but when Feeney set up a special foundation to share his good fortune with good causes, Cornell was to benefit in millions.

It was the 1987 establishment of what was initially the Atlantic Foundation which evolved into Atlantic Philanthropies that opened the valve that directed more than a billion dollars into Ireland – and for almost twenty years nobody but a select few knew where the millions were coming from.

Chuck Feeney took a special interest in the Limerick underdog of the Irish academic world but for years was the best kept secret in a country where secrets last no longer than the second person and where the inner circles of higher education re-cycle every crumb of information.

Chuck Feeney had been dabbling with bits and pieces of business in the Ireland of his ancestors from the 1970s. A family stay at Dromoland Castle in 1971 brought him into the sphere of influence of Shannon Airport which was then Ireland's sole transatlantic airport and also home to the first airport Duty Free Store. He was not only to find that he had a great deal in common with Shannon from a business point of view but that he had a soul mate in Brendan O'Regan. They shared a conviction that enterprise and doing business together was a transcending force for understanding, trust and common purpose. O'Regan had been on the front line of government thinking in that direction during his

years as chairman of the Irish Tourist Board (Bord Failte) when he laid down the groundwork for the 1960s tourism breakthrough. He was deeply influenced by his longtime mentor and giant on the Irish political scene, Sean Lemass. As the political head of

State Departments involved in economic development and later as the Taoiseach and head of government, Lemass had shared with his protégé the conviction that the surest path to re-unification of partitioned Ireland was for the Republic to outstrip Northern Ireland in economic development. In creating compelling reasons for the divided island of Ireland to see the good sense of working together, O'Regan was in the forefront of the two-pronged programme that combined tourism development with attraction of modern industry – incongruously promoting a split personality Ireland of rustic cottages and ancient castles alongside space age technologies. What mattered was that it worked and was seen to greatest advantage around Shannon under the motivating power of O'Regan. It was the sudden blooming of a modern thinking Ireland that took Sean Lemass on his sensational trip across the Border to meet and talk mutual opportunities and benefits with his Northern Ireland counterpart, Captain O'Neill. At that time scene setting by top officials was already advanced that would not only promote the two divided states of Ireland as a single tourism destination but also link up with Great Britain in tourism promotion. What would have been a momentous breakthrough and coming together in Anglo-Irish relations was lost with the 1969 outbreak of the Northern "troubles". It would take another 30 years but Brendan O'Regan lived to see the Republic of Ireland and Northern Ireland join in unified cross-Border agencies for tourism promotion as part of the Northern Ireland Peace Process. In facilitating the elaborate and labyrinthine efforts that brought about the Peace Process and its dividends, a key player was an American mystery man named Chuck Feeney.

Those bitten by the Ireland bug learn that the condition is permanent. In Chuck Feeney's case it was already in the blood. For besides the draw of ancestral roots there was much in Ireland to engage him. In a country never short of dreamers of dreams, there were people and movements driven by a relentless missionary zeal, visionaries whose perception of the big picture was limited only by frustrating dearth of resources and budding new generation initiatives like Limerick's third level college battling to cast off the stifling controls of government budget balancers. All were struggling to advance to the next stage of development in an Ireland convulsed by the escalating violence in Northern Ireland. The covert infusion of Chuck Feeney's wealth provided bridges of communication over the political minefield of Northern Ireland and provided a lift over the stumbling blocks that were holding back economic and social development. Because his booster shot intervention was invisible, and in most cases the extent of the funding was went beyond the wildest expectations what could come from donations, the dramatic advances were perceived as little Ireland coming into its own making the great leap forward on many fronts.

Once Ireland became a regular call on the round of globe-spanning travel that dominated his life, Chuck Feeney tended to buy properties. Having stayed at Ashford Castle hotel in the "Quiet Man" county Mayo settings around Cong, he agreed to take a stake in the business and subsequently was the moving spirit in bringing some of his partners into the consortium that took over the luxury lifestyle standard bearer of Irish hospitality. He toyed with the idea of an Irish home base when he thought about, but eventually decided against, buying the house in

Craughwell in county Galway which had been the home of the movie director, John Huston.

As he became more deeply involved in Irish affairs, he bought up major properties including a couple of landmark office buildings in the Dublin capital in which he provided free of charge or token rent offices for projects and programmes he supported. His Dublin property portfolio also extended to a former convent on the Monkstown residential suburb which became an Irish extension of his contribution towards thawing the Cold War that had soured East-West relations since the close of World War II. The onetime nunnery echoed to Russian and East European accents as a training centre for hand picked candidates from the former Soviet Union states brought to Ireland on scholarship programmes to familiarise them with the principles of Western capitalism and the mutual benefits of international trade and exports in breaking down barriers between peoples.

From coffers that were continually replenished by the world's depthless appetite for duty free buys, Chuck Feeny was secretly lending a helping hand to move along processes, initiatives and programmes that varied in scale from East-West global relationships to peace building on the little island homeland of his ancestors. Around Shannon and Limerick he took an interest in two Brendan O'Regan initiatives – the Co-Operation North promoter of bonding between business interests on each side of the Border between the Republic of Ireland and Northern Ireland and the spin-off Irish Peace Institute that brought third level colleges of Limerick and Northern Ireland into partnership on research, studies and exchange programmes focusing on conflict resolution and how the Irish experience could be shared in fostering understanding and reconciliation elsewhere in the world.

Where funding was the missing link between ambitions and the possible, Chuck Feeney's intervention was to provide the jump start, pump priming or short cut to what was envisioned. Characteristically, he did it his way. So in Limerick he hastened the establishment of a National Technological Park by building a hotel.

From day one of his presidency, and most probably before that, founding President, Ed Walsh envisioned that his Limerick third level college would become Ireland's MIT (Massachusetts Institute of Technology) and, like MIT, become a magnet for state of the art ventures which would knit in with the college and settle on the college campus. To map out a route to that objective, Ed Walsh turned to Tom Callanan who had been a pivotal player in establishing the Shannon Free Zone. A dynamic force and one of the old breed of what were termed practical patriots who lent their genius to building up their country and its economy rather than their own interests, Callanan had retired in the second half of the 1980s from Shannon Development where he had headed up the regional planning and economic development functions of the agency for more than 15 years. Before that he had been one of the core team of forceful personalities whose drive and openness to new ideas had been clinching factors in attracting the big name foreign enterprises that made the splash which would spill over from the Shannon Free Zone from the 1960s onwards.

Ed Walsh, who had been on the board of directors of Shannon Development from the 1970s, brought in his fellow Corkman and tasked him to lead and co-ordinate a plan that would fit out the Limerick third level college as a 21st century university.

It became known as the "Twenty Ten" project and the idea was to tap into every possible pool of intelligence, knowhow and experience to draw up an action agenda and infrastructure inventory of what would serve as the key features that would give the Limerick a competitive advantage in attracting the best around in every sense – students, researchers and the most advanced and sophisticated enterprises – in the year 2010. Callanan and Walsh could see it all happening on a technological park that would take shape on the 600 acres around the college. Sights were set higher than another technology park. The vision was for a National Technological Park.

The concept of assembling a virtually irresistible "everything you ever wanted in a location for enterprise" package centred on the Limerick college was calculated to defy government and its apparatus as well as a predictable phalanx of negative influences to stand in the way of the Limerick ambition. Chuck Feeney, who had demonstrated his special interest when flying in crates of champagne for the celebration when a University of Limerick was proclaimed in September 1989, did not hide his support.

Ed Walsh had confided in Chuck Feeney his disquiet about the future use of a tract of land that lay directly across the road from the entrance to the new university. His concern was that the prime piece of property would become the setting for a development that would be out of keeping with the vision that the university had for the area.

Chuck Feeney quietly bought the property and promptly donated the land to the university and then put in a bid to buy a site on the property for a hotel which would give the university a handsome return for a slice of the land it had received as a gift. And from Chuck Feeney there was more. He built a hotel with a difference which was also a hotel that would make a difference. That would make all the difference in bringing the concept of a National Technological Park to fruition.

The Castletroy Park Hotel was an expression of modern Limerick, the shabby old city which was rousing itself for yet another make-over in which the new University of Limerick and its ideas-spinning President were as usual in the thick of the action. At 12 million Irish Punts (€ 15.25million) the imposing new landmark represented an enormous vote of confidence in Limerick and what its new university was going about. As a standard bearer for Limerick, the hotel was second only to the new Conrad Hotel in Dublin as the biggest investment in the country's hospitality and leisure sector. Most of all the hotel proclaimed Limerick as an Information Age trail blazer. Matching up to its quality peaks in interior design, facilities and operation, the Castletroy Park Hotel was also tuned into and wired into the most advanced technologies that were then making the world a much smaller place in communication terms. By laying on state of the art technology, Chuck Feeney was doing yet another double favour for Limerick and its university. To the scouting teams from prospecting corporations lured to Limerick by the competitive advantage appeal of the embryonic National Technological Park, the sophistication of the hotel and its high-speed communications epitomised that Limerick was on the move into the 21st century and setting the pace. By his insistence on showpiece standards of communications technologies, Chuck Feeney locked the State utility and promotion agencies into the initiative and his hotel also forced their hand in laying on the prime infrastructure of networks and systems which would be the making of the National Technological Park.

A hotel venture was not taking Chuck Feeney into uncharted waters. While making his fortune in related fields, he kept in touch with his university alma mater of Cornell University – where his "giving while living" started when he was asked for a donation of one thousand dollars and gave ten thousand. In economically stressed Ireland of the 1980s he helped prop up the hospitality industry by setting up a scholarship programme which took young Irish hotel management personnel on work experience with practitioners within the top tiers of the American hotel sector. Before the Castletroy Park he had also bought a hotel on the other side of the country, at Woodenbridge in county Wicklow. The Cornell connection was invoked yet again when he appointed Cornell graduate Padraig Berry to head up the holding company into which the Castletroy Park in Limerick would be slotted and typical of the Feeney style of subtle stamping of his commitment, the company was registered as EGB (the "Erin Go Breath" catchword or toast of Irish freedom movements).

In elevating Limerick to new status as home to one of a handful of top hotels in Ireland and one that could hold its own in international quality standards, the advent of the Castletroy Park Hotel was spot on in its timing. The 1991 official opening of the hotel by the President of Ireland, Mrs. Mary Robinson, was one of the milestone events in a twelve months calendar of headline happenings organised to raise the profile of Limerick city at national and international levels. The 300th anniversary of the Treaty of Limerick which brought to a close a 2-year siege and the last war of European kings with armies drawn from all corners of Europe had been picked out as an ideal backdrop for promoting the "new Limerick" then taking shape from a series of renewal initiatives hatched by state agencies and private investors to transform the city. That "Treaty 300" programme also brought to light a long-standing shortcoming of the city which was finally rectified by the combination of Chuck Feeney, Ed Walsh and the University of Limerick.

The comprehensively representative partnership of State, civic, academic, business and voluntary bogies and agencies involved in putting the "Treaty 300" programme together had been planning for three years. City native and then the tourism product development manager at Shannon Development, Gerry Lowe had been drafted in on secondment as overall Director and had assembled a team that worked with eleven committees involved in staging events from world Irish dancing championships to world premieres of new musical compositions. An inbuilt frustration throughout the build-up and planning phase as well as the actual rolling out of the 1991 programme was the lack of a performance venue in the city. The venerable City Theatre and the landmark Savoy Cinema that seated a thousand or more in the mass movie-going era before television were now memories but had not been replaced and the city's Belltable Arts Centre was home to what amounted to a miniature theatre. Director Lowe and the various organising groups had to improvise and at times compromise on quality standards when highbrow Treaty 300 recitals and concerts were staged in a former dance hall that had also served as a temporary home for an electronics assembly operation and even, with a dispensation for the occasion, the city's Redemptorist Church. A proper performance venue worthy of the city of Limerick was a recurring theme in speeches, statements and debates with promises and pledges aplenty from city council officialdom and from elected representatives at local and national levels. From all sides there were calls on the city administration and its planners to make a dedicated performance venue a priority. Ed Walsh did not join the clamour demanding action from others. He simply commented that the University of Limerick would take on the task. With the limitless largesse of Chuck Feeney as the secret ingredient, he did just that.

The result was the standout Foundation Building which housed the University of Limerick Concert Hall, a performance space that cupped a seated audience of over 1,000 in its intimate embrace and with acoustics that established the venue as ready-made for live broadcast transmissions from day one. In shaping the concert hall, Chuck Feeney brought in an eminent New York architect, Bob Fox, to advise local Limerick developer Pat Whelan and his BDP construction company.

Besides the prestige of its fabulous new venue, the UL Concert Hall would be a catalyst in lifting Limerick to new international status as a cultural and academic centre. The combination of university and concert hall helped college President Ed Walsh to lure the innovative young composer and professor of music, Micheal O Suilleabhain from what was then University College Cork to lead the new World Music Centre to new horizons in traditional music and dance. In turn, the energy and vision inherent in the marriage of the most modern university in the country with deeply rooted native culture and tradition were compelling factors in the decision of the Irish Chamber Orchestra to decentralise and relocate to Limerick and make the UL campus its home.

Whenever pressing needs or bright new ideas and projects requiring a funding push start cropped up, the boundless support of Chuck Feeney continued to flow to the University of Limerick under the "giving while living" disbursement of his fortune of more than four billion dollars. Having provided catch up support for the underdog Limerick university, Chuck Feeney's Atlantic Philanthropies pumped untold but undisclosed millions into the Irish academic system. Described by Ireland's Nobel Prize winning poet Seamus Heaney as "epoch making", the intervention of the Atlantic Foundation was estimated to have reinforced the Irish economy with donations in excess of $1.25billion from which at least $750million was life support to innovation, enterprise and initiatives in third level education.

Brendan O'Regan: *Irishman with American Vision*

The ideas has been crowding his firecracker imagination for years but it took a six week tour through the United States and a stately sea voyage home for Brendan O'Regan to set out the giant steps which brought Ireland onto the world tourism map.

A favourite with the government administration in the persons of its most powerful ministers and, significantly, its top officials, O'Regan was chosen as one of the four representatives from Ireland who joined a sixteen-strong group on a familiarisation tour of the hotel and leisure industry in the United States. It was 1950 and the old and new worlds of Europe and the USA were in the process of settling back after the upheaval, trauma and turmoil of World War II. Yet Europe and the United States had been brought closer together in more ways than as allies against the Axis powers. Hostilities in the European theatre and the aftermath which saw a substantial US military presence making camp on the Rhine meant that a new generation and social layer of American society were aware of and interested in Europe. The enormous advances that the imperative of rapid movement had brought to aviation during the war had also revolutionized air travel which was being brought within the range of a mass market. The American families that were splashing out ten billion dollars on vacations each year were beginning to move out and seek new experiences. But less than one in twenty of the 23million American families that took vacations actually ventured outside the border of their homeland. Going into the new decade of the Fifties, three quarters of those who went outside the United States for their holidays headed to Canada, with Mexico and Cuba next in line with shares of 10 per cent and 5 per cent respectively. Europe got half of the remainder.

In stumbling out of the wreckage of its second world conflict in thirty years, Europe was being rebuilt with most substantial help from the United States. The Marshall Plan for European regeneration put together by General George Marshall was turning a blueprint into the realities of physical renewal with a massive infusion of American dollars.

It was so that an American public becoming more adventurous in vacation choices could share in the experience of what American aid was doing for Europe and also to stimulate activity for civil aviation on a global scale that the hand-picked sixteen from key areas of the hospitality sector in Europe were brought on an intensive round of visits to bring them face to face with what the on-vacation American traveller was accustomed to and the standards that would be demanded to attract Americans and their dollars across the Atlantic.

The impact of that trip on Brendan O'Regan is most vividly illustrated by two actions. Even then a man of enormous influence reaching to the top levels of policy-making and direction in Ireland, he was nevertheless a man of few written words. Throughout decades of government service he was never one for lengthy submissions or documents or for that matter in communicating by memorandum. Yet, the American tour in the first half of 1950 prompted him to assemble a closely typed document running to 41 pages. Such was the importance that he attached to setting down a detailed record of what he had learned that he made his way back to Ireland on a transatlantic liner. It was on the "SS America" that the seeds of an Irish tourism industry were planted in the most fertile of brains.

He was not supposed to bring back recommendations. But he did and in great detail. Before his departure, government officials gave the four Irish delegates on the group strict instructions that what was expected from them was a report recording the tour details. But the bureaucrats were adamant, in the case of O'Regan especially, that there were to be "no recommendations".

Brendan O'Regan defied the instructions. He was in a position to do so and the government officials knew and feared that only too well. From the latter half of the 1930s when he was plucked from the relative obscurity of managing a west of Ireland hotel and entrusted with a task in the front line of Irish international relations, Brendan O'Regan had the ear and the trust of the most powerful figures in government. His political mentor was Sean Lemass who nursed and fortified the Irish economy through bleak decades of anaemia during service in the key economic ministry before reinvigorating the country with a State-led surge of confidence when he attained party and government leadership. O'Regan was also the protégé of

John Leydon, the department secretary and right hand man to Lemass whose diminutive stature perfectly disguised the enormous power he wielded at the centre of a web of State initiatives and ventures.

It was at the prompting of John Leydon that minister Lemass appointed O'Regan to run the restaurant at the Foynes flying boat base when Ireland's wartime neutrality meant that the incumbent management from British Overseas Airways Corporation had to withdraw. At the highest level of government there was full appreciation that the connection to transatlantic aviation at Foynes was moving Ireland into a new and elite sphere which would put the country in a most searching international spotlight. The classiest person they knew to take on the job was Brendan O'Regan. Their trust was not only rewarded but brought in dividends for the State. In his Foynes appointment the commission to O'Regan was to make the most favourable impression possible. O'Regan did just that and also made profits and when land planes moved the transatlantic stopover to Shannon Airport, it started the built up of what became the biggest employment centre in the west of Ireland with 1,000 employees in an empire that delivered profits in every year of operation.

In bolstering enterprise and jobs in the impoverished west of Ireland which in turn shaped government policy confining transatlantic flights to the Shannon gateway, the Sales & Catering Service headed by O'Regan featured prominently in government thinking and planning. Top government officials would acknowledge in later years that when proposals or new projects came up the line from Shannon, resistance or reservations were pointless. Anything that emanated from O'Regan was going to get the go-ahead.

O'Regan was the outstanding innovator in the Irish hospitality sector. So he was an automatic choice for the Marshall Plan trip to the United States. Also included in the Irish quartet was Patrick F. Dornan, who held an eminent place in the Irish hotel industry of the time. He was manager of the flagship and pride of the State-owned Great Southern Hotel chain which operated the only Grade A hotels outside of the Dublin capital. The Great Southern hotels were a subsidiary of the State-run railways and had followed the rail network to the centres of outstanding visitor appeal among which the Parknasilla Great Southern in county Kerry managed by Patrick Dornan was the jewel in the crown. Patrick Dornan also broke ranks in defying government instructions and he co-signed the recommendations and document submitted on April 29th, 1950.

The tour of America made a startling impact on two counts. The eyes of O'Regan and the others in the party were opened to the enormous range of accommodation facilities that Americans were accustomed to. For O'Regan and the Irish contingent, there was the shock of the gaping black hole of ignorance and disinformation about Ireland. It was not simply a matter that information about Ireland was skimpy. For the major tour operations of the time, Ireland might as well have been non-existent. In a time when Cooks Tours was the market leader, its 39 escorted Grand Tours of Europe not only bypassed Ireland completely but the long established last port of call on the westward voyage at Cobh or Queenstown did not even figure on the lists of European ports. Ireland was also out in the cold when checks were made on the itineraries of other operators of European tours. "Simmons Gateway" tours offered no less than 87 options for seeing Europe and the operator of the Polytechnic range of tours had 12 different packages. None included or mentioned Ireland.

The blank or distorted levels of knowledge concerning Ireland became shockingly clear when guide books and other promotional materials available to prospective travellers were examined. The "Guide to Europe" from the respected New York Herald Tribune publishers devoted 33 pages to Belgium, 14 to Holland and 3 to Ireland. The accuracy and sources of clearly un-checked information in the Herald Tribune guide were also very questionable. Included in the 1949/50 edition was the statement –"only three people have actually kissed the Blarney Stone in the past 30 years". Doubts that the compiler of the Ireland information had actually been in the country were prompted by the statement –"In the mountains of County Joyce are tweeds and flocks of sheep" and the depiction of the Irish capital was not calculated to send Americans rushing to see for themselves. "There is desperate poverty in the streets of Dublin" was hardly a recommendation to the prospective visitor. The shock experienced by O'Regan had already been experienced by the staff of America's top travel magazine when they published an article on Ireland which also projected a warped image of the Emerald Isle. On a visit to the Curtis Publishing Company, the editors of the 800,000 a month circulation "Holiday Magazine" told O'Regan that they had been "quite astounded" by what for them was an unexpected and unfavourable reaction to what readers regarded as misrepresentations of Ireland. From the sophisticated American publishing sector, another lesson was learned when it emerged that promotion of travel to Ireland was being held back restricted by the total absence of colour pictures.

Although he had been running and developing the catering and sales operations of a State airport for the previous seven years, Brendan O'Regan was a hotelier at heart. When his farmer-cum-businessman father bought The Old Ground Hotel in the county Clare capital of Ennis, the family would be taken on Continental holidays and the youngsters sent on scouting missions to pick up tips from the leading hotels and restaurants. Earmarked to run the family hotel, Brendan had been sent for training in London, France, Germany and Switzerland and it was the reputation he was rapidly building as manager of The Falls Hotel in the spa town of Ennistymon in his native county that his outstanding talent was spotted by the leading figures in government. Therefore it was predictable that he and fellow hotelier, Patrick Dornan were struck by just how much ground Ireland would have to make up if the country was to entertain ambitions to entice American travellers to the Emerald Isle.

It was equally predictable that more than half of the 41 pages of their joint report and submissions focused on the dramatic transformation that would be required of the hotel sector in Ireland.

In precise detail, the two hotel professionals put together a document which set out the general specifications of what an American visitor would expect and demand of hotel facilities. Setting new benchmarks were the requirements for toilet, bath or shower facilities to adjoin each room, for twin beds to be the standard rather than the double, heating to be at a standard 70 degrees Fahrenheit and for room service to be on call from a phone connection in each bedroom. Every detail was covered – from reception desk skills and layout to accounting and adoption of American standards in compiling accounts and extending down to the finest details of bedroom décor, fittings and furnishings.

From the vast range of hotel facilities that the group experienced and visited, O'Regan was particularly taken by the motel and also by self catering cottage court accommodations which he saw as models that could well be replicated in Ireland.

In the course of their introduction to the inner workings of a broad range of hotel operations representative of the 15,000 hotels operating in the USA of 1950, the two hoteliers recognised that training at all levels was of the utmost importance in keeping the hospitality industry on its toes. They knew that back in Ireland the same view was shared by leading members of the Irish Hotel Federation who had floated an idea for jointly funding a hotel management training programme. While the idea had not taken root the O'Regan-Dornan report cited a hotel management school as a priority need, so much so that a pledge was included that if the industry or government did not take the initiative, Shannon Airport would take on the task.

Very much aware of the heritage and scenic splendour that Ireland had to offer, O'Regan and Dornan were greatly impressed by the restoration and re-enactment initiatives at locations including the development of Williamsburg, Virginia as a visitor attraction. Their report suggested that similar projects could showcase the then untapped heritage appeal of Ireland for the American visitor and identified Bunratty Castle near Shannon Airport as a ready-made opportunity.

The fastidious attention to detail that set them apart as outstanding practitioners in their profession was evident in every paragraph of their observations but in its overview the document stands out as a blueprint for the subsequent development and growth of tourism to Ireland.

They set out a vision for transformation of Ireland's hotel sector from charming but shabby old world dignity to the contemporary standards of the New World. As a signal to the world travel industry that Ireland was going after American tourism business in a professional manner, a new 200-250 bedroom hotel in Dublin was put forward as the standard bearer and standard setter. Elsewhere in the country they envisioned that established hotels would build on new wings that would lift bedroom and other facilities to levels that matched up to US standards. Acutely conscious of the dearth of investment capital in Ireland, they suggested a series of supports and aids that could be made available especially at government discretion. The taxation reliefs on capital investment and low interest loans suggested in the report would be included alongside non-repayable grant support in the years when Brendan O'Regan was serving on the Irish Tourist Board (Bord

Failte), as its youngest member from 1955 and Chairman of the Board of Directors from 1957 to 1972.

America had brought them face to face with a tomorrow's world of travel that made O'Regan and Dornan heralds of the shape of the hospitality industry that had to come about if Ireland was to make the American visitor feel at home. They extended their alert call to sectors beyond their familiar hotel and catering areas of expertise, putting the transport sector on notice that American standards of comfort would be needed in tour coaches and that self-drive car hire was a must for an American society in which the automobile was a fixture.

The timing of their study-familiarisation tour was especially significant for Brendan O'Regan. In the facts and figures presented to the group, they learned that the previous year had marked a milestone in transatlantic travel as 1949 was the year in which air travel exceeded passenger movements by sea. Even though Ireland was being bypassed by both air and sea travellers, O'Regan could see that the dramatic reduction in travelling time would bring travel to Europe within the range of income groups for whom crossing the Atlantic by ocean liner would have

been out of the question. The era of mass market travel by air between continents was dawning and with it the opportunity of all time for O'Regan's Shannon Airport.

The Shannon agenda that was conceived with Marshal Plan support, gestated on the US study tour, took shape on the "SS America" ocean liner return journey and delivered with multiple helping American hands at Shannon Airport, was the starting point of a mission. The O'Regan-Dornan report set out an action programme that would get into its stride almost immediately and gain momentum through the 1950s decade with the origination of a series of innovations that would open Ireland to twofold enrichment from the United States – through tourism and industrial investment.

The Shannon initiatives that flowed from the Marshall Plan tour included:

- The take off to world leadership by the Shannon Duty Free Store. As an incentive to air traffic, Shannon had been declared a Duty Free Airport in 1947. It was on the return journey to Ireland from the Marshall Plan study tour as a passenger on the "SS America" that Brendan O'Regan recognised the revenue potential of a shop operating outside the taxation net. The availability of tax-free merchandise through the on-board shop did not have significant appeal to passengers, but O'Regan calculated that an airport point of departure would offer much greater convenience – for purchases on the last leg of a journey; for last minute gift and other bargain buys and for occupying time for passengers awaiting their plane connection. Up to that point the airport shop at Shannon had been no more than a kiosk selling souvenirs and local handcrafts. Until then sales of liquor at the duty-free prices allowed within the Shannon zone had been restricted to airline crews. But the eye-opening experience on the "SS America" was the starting point for first duty-free airport store in the world. With a spectacular expansion of the merchandise range, Shannon Duty Free became the export-promoting showcase for Waterford Crystal, Irish linens and tweeds, Aran Island knitwear and Beleek china which took their place alongside the finest of French perfumery, Italian fashion wear, Swiss watches plus top of the range jewelery and cameras. The immediate success of the Shannon Duty Free spawned the establishment of Shannon Mail Order which from 1954 became a major dollar earner and commercial success for Shannon and the Irish economy.

- The Shannon College of Hotel Management was the first of its kind in Ireland and became a reality within a year of the proposal set out in the O'Regan-Dornan report. The college enrolled its first students in the autumn of 1951 to become the source of the "Shannon trained" graduates who have distinguished themselves in leading hotels around the globe and brought lustre to Irish hospitality with the combination of natural charm and polished professionalism in which the blossoming of Irish tourism was rooted.

- Bunratty Castle, the finest example of 15th century building expertise to be found in Ireland, was not only restored when Brendan O'Regan convinced the British nobleman, Lord Gort, to forsake his plan to buy the ancestral castle near Gort and rebuild Bunratty instead. Lord Gort also fitted out the castle in the authentic style of the period with his personal collection of furnishings, tapestries and works of art. The restored castle opened to the public in 1960, became the setting for the castle banquets and entertainment that captivated the American travelling public and became the hub for Bunratty Folk Park and associated castle and attraction developments.

- The motels and roadside inns that made a major impression on Brendan O'Regan were also introduced to Ireland as a direct result of the Marshall Plan tour. With his belief that he would see Bunratty Castle restored and brought back to life, O'Regan identified and personally bought a site in the shadow of the castle where his hotelier instincts told him a hotel could be sympathetically fitted into the local landscape without impinging on the overall air of antiquity around Bunratty. He did not follow through with his hotel plan but instead sold the site and paved the way for American investment in the Irish hotel sector when businessman Al McCarthy opened the Shannon Shamrock Inn which was built in record time for its opening in August 1959.

- On the basis of what they had seen in the United States, the O'Regan-Dornan combination made a point of urging a government initiative which would locate an office in the United States to promote travel to Ireland. Their report stressed that the initiative should be headed by an Irish person with a feel for the country and the depth of knowledge that was found to be astoundingly lacking during the US study tour. Yet again, Shannon took the initiative. O'Regan sent out not one but two emissaries. The impact that the pair made is reflected in what followed – Bill Maxwell was to become the Aer Lingus public relations manager for North America and subsequently head the Publicity and PR function for the national airline while Patricia Barry would be head hunted to first head up the sales and later become general manager and a share holder in the Dromoland Castle Hotel.

- The "cottage court" concept outlined in the O'Regan-Dornan report which envisioned the romantic rustic charm of the white-walled Irish cottage and thatch roofing being combined with modern comforts including underfloor heating, fully fitted bathrooms and all electric kitchens would not become a reality until 1969. But the launch of Rent-an-Irish Cottage was a masterstroke in spreading American tourism in particular to rural village communities and set the standards as a precursor of the self-catering tourist developments that would spring up across the country in the decades that followed.

The Marshall Plan tour was instrumental in setting in motion the series of inter-locking and inter-dependent initiatives and schemes that won Shannon Airport recognition at home and abroad as a hotbed of innovation that showed Irish flair and imagination at its best.

For Ireland and Irish tourism, but especially for Shannon Airport and the west of Ireland generally, Brendan O'Regan was not so much the ideas man but the man who made ideas work. For his country, his government, his home place and his airport, and then for the Americans who had the good fortune to encounter an extraordinary human being, Brendan O'Regan was the right man in the right place and at the crucially right time. As Brendan O'Regan himself would observe –he was also the man who, when opportunity came knocking, was the epitome of "right man, right place – and ready"

STARS FROM THE SKIES

Mary Pickford

Forget modern-day movie megastars and the fortunes they command – Mary Pickford left them all in the shade in every way, audience pulling-power, earning power and business power. She captivated cinema audiences and was dubbed "America's Sweetheart" in 75 silent era melodrama features turned out over a three year period. She started as a $40 a week player in 1909 but by 1913 commanded $500 a week and three years later was earning over $500,000 a year. In just one year she was the title role star of "Poor Little Rich Girl"; "The Little American"; "Rebecca of Sunnybrook Farm" and "The Little Princess" – all released in 1917. Two years later she was a trail blazer when joining with Charlie Chaplin and the swashbuckling hear-throb, Douglas Fairbanks who became her second husband, in forming the independent United Artists production company. Under that banner, she was the original "Pollyanna" and "Tess of the

Mrs. Buddy Rogers, better known as Mary Pickford the world's sweetheart.

Storm Country" and at age 29 she played the title role of a boy and also the role of his mother in the movie "Little Lord Fontleroy". She won an Oscar for "Coquette" in 1929 and when she was pictured at Shannon, she had been married since 1937 to Charles "Buddy" Rogers, who won the first silent movie Oscar for "Wings" in 1927.

Broderick Crawford

Burly "tough guy" actor, Broderick Crawford had hit and miss film and television careers which touched heights of acclaim and popularity but was largely type-cast in "heavy" roles in run-of-the mill movies. Born in Philadelphia to vaudeville performer parents, at age 26 he made his Broadway breakthrough as the simpleton Lenny in John Steinbeck's "Of Mice and Men". Even though he was signed up by Hollywood two years later in 1939, he lost the Lenny role in the movie version to Lon Chaney Jr. who was limited to similar casting for the rest of his screen career. Crawford would appear in average movies for ten years before winning a best actor Academy Award as the corrupt politician in "All the Kings Men". He followed up with another major hit a year later when he played a self-made scrap iron tycoon in "Born Yesterday" which won Judy Holliday the best actress Oscar. Dubbed "difficult" to work with, the remainder of his screen career was unremarkable. He was back in a starring lead role in the television series "Highway Patrol", playing "Chief" Dan Mathews for the entire 1955-59 run of the popular police drama. He died of a stroke in 1986.

John Mills

Quiet heroes were personified in English cinema by John Mills whose 60 year career in over 100 films would win him a 1976 knighthood. A film with an Irish story and setting, "Ryan's Daughter" marked a career pinnacle when he won a 1970 Best Actor Oscar for his portrayal of the mute village idiot, Michael. In an earlier Irish-themed production, he played a reluctant IRA gunman in "The Gentle Gunman" (1952). On stage from his teenage years, he was spotted by the celebrated Noel Coward who cast him in a number of London productions and also in the World War II flag-waver "In Which We Serve" which had two giants of stage and screen, Coward and David Lean, behind the cameras. Two career milestones for John Mills were to be with David Lean. He played the mature Pip in the 1946 production of "Great Expectations" and would

link up with Lean again 24 years later in "Ryan's Daughter". He married novelist Mary Hayley Bell in 1943. Their daughters also took to the stage, with Juliet the first to follow father in a stage and film career and younger sister Hayley was a major child star who returned in television drama in her adult years. John Mills died in 2005 aged 97.

Danny Kaye

In 50 years as an actor, comic, singer, and mimic Danny Kaye was a box-office winner on cinema screens, in the 1960s heyday of US television and as a singer with a special appeal to children.

Born David Daniel Kaminsky in Brooklyn, New York in 1913, his drew on his parents' background as immigrants from the Ukraine when adopting a Russian accent to make his early mark with tongue-twisting routines and monologues. He reflected his Jewish heritage in outstanding screen performances in a Golden Globe award winning "Me and the Colonel" (1959) and much later as a Holocaust survivor in the 1981 television special "Skokie".

In a variety of cinema roles he brought James Thurber's immortal day-dreamer to life in "The Secret World of Walter Mitty" (1947); played Hans Christian Anderson" from which a string of recording hits ensued and portrayed the jazz

pioneer, Red Nichols in "The Five Pennies" (1959).

A 1955 honorary Academy Award was followed by a 1964 Emmy for his television show and his work as the first International Ambassador for the United Nation's children's fund, UNICEF, was recognised with a Jean Hersholt Humanitarian Award five years before his death in 1987.

James Stewart

At Shannon with his wife Gloria who shared his life for 45 years, James Stewart was on familiar ground. An aviator in private life, he set up an Arizona flying school that trained 200,000 war-time airmen and became a flying instructor when he was the first major American movie star to enlist when the US entered World War II. At Shannon too he was following in the footsteps of the transatlantic solo flight pioneer who he portrayed in "The Spirit of St. Louis". Charles Lindbergh had taken part in the survey that picked out the site for the first stop in Europe when the fledgling Irish state decided to take off with the air age. An architect before turning to acting, Jimmy Stewart typified the American hero – from small town family man to rugged frontiersman and from fresh faced innocent to hard-boiled detective. Unfailingly impersonated with a slow talking drawl, it was as a fast talking reporter that he won his 1940 Oscar in "The

Philadelphia Story" which was remade with music as "High Society". In 60 years before the cameras he was a favourite leading man for legendary directors, Frank Kapra, Alfred Hitchcock, Billy Wilder and John Ford. He died aged 89 in 1997.

Barry Fitzgerald

Thanks to "ET" becoming a 1980s fan and to television repeats, the most lasting memory of Barry Fitzgerald on celluloid is of the elfin (or more appropriately leprechaun-like) jarvey-cum-matchmaker in "The Quiet Man". And while it was also John Ford who cast him in his first film role in the 1936 adaptation of the classic O'Casey drama "The Plough and The Stars", it was not as a stage Irishman that the actor born William Shields made his most impressive marks in the cinema. While he would win a 1944 Supporting Actor Oscar when he and Bing Crosbie played priests in "Going My Way", he was comfortable in the zany Hepburn-Grant comedy "Bringing Up Baby"; in the Welsh mining village drama "How Green Was My Valley" in which he again teamed up with John Ford and as the central detective character in the ground-breaking "The Naked City" which brought movie-making onto the streets for the first time in 1948. He had adopted a stage name to distinguish him from his actor brother, Arthur Shields. They were Abbey actors together before both taking to Hollywood and both featured in "The Quiet Man" with Arthur playing the village rector. Born in 1888, Barry Fitzgerald died in 1961.

Mel Ferrer

Although he appeared in over 80 movies and was behind the cameras in up to a dozen more, Mel Ferrer is best remembered for his 14 year marriage to Audrey Hepburn. He starred with his wife in "War and Peace", directed her in "Green Mansions" and produced the hit "Wait Until Dark" thriller the year before they divorced in 1968. Born Melchior Gaston Ferrer, his mother was a New York socialite and his Cuban father a surgeon. On stage from teenage years the drop-out from Princeton University took many career paths that finally led to a life in films. He was a chorus dancer on Broadway at 21 before being struck down with polio. He later built a highly successful radio career as a producer-director before returning to Broadway and into motion pictures from 1947. Six feet three inches tall with aristocratic good looks, he was a busy screen actor through the 1950s and 60s before turning to Europe where he appeared in a string of forgettable films. He also worked in television where he is best remembered for his role opposite Jane Wyman in the highly successful "Falcon Crest" series of the 1980s. He announced his official retirement from acting in 1997 – on his 80th birthday.

Adolphe Menjou

When stopping off at Shannon, dapper Adolphe Menjou who made a 50 year cinema career out of playing Continental types, was on the home ground of his Connemara

mother Anna Joyce. But his debonair style and appearance was inherited from his father who was of French extraction. Born in 1890 and acting from college years he was in movies from 1916. He co-starred with Rudolph Valentino in "The Sheik"; with Mary Pickford in "Through the Back Door" and in the silent version of "The Three Musketeers", all in 1921. After lean years with the coming of "talkies" he was back as a 1930 headliner opposite Marlene Dietrich and Gary Cooper in "Morocco". The following year he was nominated for a best actor Oscar when teamed with Pat O'Brien in the original version of "The Front Page". He was also in a lead role in the original 1937 version of "A Star Is Born" opposite Janet Gaynor and Fredric March. A committed anti-Communist, his 1947 co-operation with the Joe McCarthy witch-hunt hearings contributed to the tapering off of his cinema career. Yet one of his most memorable roles was in the 1957 "Paths of Glory" as a corrupt French general. He died in 1963.

Johnnie Ray

Johnnie Ray, Crooner, photographed at the Tourist Bureau.

He was the teen idol of his day and the popular music bridge between the swing era when Frank Sinatra was the craze and the Elvis Presley rock and roll revolution of the late 1950s. Johnnie Ray brought music mania and teen frenzy into the front pages when his record-breaking run at the London Palladium had the bobby-soxers of the time swooning, screaming and also sobbing along with the star. Decades before The Who smashed up their equipment on stage, Johnnie Ray was beating up his piano, writhing on the floor and crying. He was dubbed "the prince of wails" in the tabloid press that churned out a non-stop flow of lurid reports many of which were later acknowledged as smears. From Hopewell, Oregon, his rhythm-based style of singing at Detroit night spots won him a recording contract. He was an overnight sensation when his double-sided hit "Cry" and his own composition "The Little White Cloud That Cried" sold a million. Successive hits followed through the 1950s. Partially deaf from an accident at age 13, unsuccessful 1958 surgery which left him almost totally deaf contributed to the eclipse of his star. He died aged 63 in 1990.

Eartha Kitt

The original sex kitten whose purring voice in speech and song made her the sensation of the Paris cabaret scene in the 1950s, her recordings of "Under the Bridges of Paris" and "Just an Old Fashioned Girl" became standards. Described as "the most exciting girl in the world" by cinema genius, Orson Welles, the very limited opportunities for black performers confined her celebrated talents to the theatre and concert stage until she clawed her way into television legend playing "Catwoman" in the tongue-in-cheek "Batman" series. Turning 40 during the 1966-68 run of the "Batman" series, she remained a statuesque 35-23-35. An illegitimate child of the South Carolina cotton fields who was abandoned by her mother, the school drop-out who lived rough in New York before getting her break on the stage was an outspoken nonconformist. She became a virtual outcast from the United States following anti-Vietnam War comments at a White House function and also enraged her own race by performing in South Africa during the apartheid regime. Her enduring talent was marked by Tony Award nominations for Broadway

performances 22 years apart, for best actress in 1978 and for a featured role in a musical in 2000. She was performing the splits on television chat shows during a European tour just weeks before her death at age 81 during Christmas 2008.

Kenneth More

Bright and breezy English actor Kenneth More was at home in adventure, light comedy and wartime drama films and equally comfortable in leading man or support roles. Yet he came to acting and the screen from the wings of the celebrated Windmill Theatre and its nude tableaux. At 17 he was turned down for the RAF and turned back from Canada where ambitions to be a fur trapper were dashed because he had no immigration papers. Windmill Theatre supremo, Vivian Van Damm, gave him a backstage job and he progressed to the stage playing straight man feed to the cream of British comedians who got their break at the theatre. Wartime action with the Royal Navy interrupted his career in stage productions which he resumed from 1946 and was a virtual fixture in 1950s British films. He made a big impression as the cocky rival in "Genevieve" and was awarded a BAFTA as best newcomer in the first of a highly successful movie series in "Doctor In the House". He was also a central character in the 1967 milestone "Forsyte Saga" television series which continues on public television channels throughout the world. Commemorated by the Kenneth More Theatre in Ilford, Essex, he died in 1982 aged 67.

Merle Oberon

With a background and screen career to rival the most far-fetched movie script, Merle Oberon left indelible marks on the film industry. Born in India to mixed-race parents, she rose from an impoverished childhood to get a start in British films as a teenager. Estelle Merle O'Brien Thompson was working as a nightclub hostess and bit part film actress when she caught the eye of renowned film director, Alexander Korda. He changed her name from Queenie O'Brien to Merle Oberon when casting her as Anne Boleyn opposite the legendary Charles Laughton in "The Private Life of Henry VIII" and two years later was a 1935 Oscar winner for "The Dark Angel". She starred in "The Scarlet Pimpernel" and was to co-star opposite Laughton again in the unfinished "I Claudius" which was abandoned when she was scarred in a serious auto crash. But, thanks to skilled lighting, she returned to films to play the role of "Cathy" in "Wuthering Heights" (1939) and would make over 20 further films up to the mid 1950s. She was Lady Korda before her

1939 divorce from the knighted director and was married to her fourth husband when she died aged 68 in 1979.

Diana Lynn

Her child prodigy gifts as a pianist brought her into movies in 1939 and she was featured under her own name of Dolores Marie Loehr before the Paramount studio decided to develop her acting talent and changed her name to Diana Lynn for her juvenile comedy role in

"The Major and the Minor" with Ginger Rogers. She was a big draw throughout the 1940s, making up to four films a year. She was an early success in "The Miracle of Morgan's Creek" released in 1944 and she finished off the decade in the "My Friend Irma" comedy hit which introduced cinema audiences to the Dean Martin and Jerry Lewis partnership that went on to enormous 1950s popularity. They reprised their roles in the "My Friend Irma Goes West" sequel but Diana Lynn's star went into decline in the 1950s when her most notable role was in the much lampooned "Bedtime for Bonzo" opposite the future President of the United States, Ronald Reagan. She made a cinema comeback after a 15 year break in which she was running a New York travel agency and was preparing for a new role when she suffered a stroke and died nine days later in 1971.

Sylva Koscina

Born in Yugoslavia in 1933, she was a teenage beauty queen in her adopted home of Italy to where her family had fled at the end of World War II. She progressed from fashion model into Italian movies from the mid-1950s and came to international attention as co-star in the highly successful "Hercules" epics starring the former "Mr. Universe" muscle man Steve Reeves. During the 1960s and early 70s she was starring in British and US productions opposite established stars Dirk Bogarde "Hot Enough for June" (1964); with Richard Johnson in the "Bulldog Drummond" revival "Deadlier Than the Male" (1966); Paul Newman in "The Secret War of Harry Frigg" (1967) David McCallum "Three Bites of the Apple" (1967) and Kirk Douglas "A Lovely Way to Die" (1968). She was back on the Italian movie scene opposite Rock Hudson in the war-drama "Hornet's Nest" in 1970. Thereafter her film roles were sporadic and posing nude at the age of 42 for the Italian edition of Playboy" in 1975 failed to revive her cinema career. She enjoyed a successful Italian stage career in the 1980s. She died at the age of 61 in 1994, the year in which her last movie "Kim Novak Is on the Phone" was released.

Edmond O'Brien

Making a Shannon stop rather than the passing through stopovers of other VIPs during aircraft re-fuelling, Oscar winner Edmond O'Brien was arriving for a holiday in Ireland with his wife, the former Olga San Juan. On stage from his college years, he acted with the Mercury Theatre of Orson Welles before making his cinema debut in the 1939 production of "The Hunchback of Notre Dame". After World War II service, he built a career as a popular supporting actor and won his Best Supporting Actor Academy Award for his publicity agent portrayal in "The Barefoot Contessa" starring screen idols of the day Humphrey Bogart and Ava Gardner. Ten years later he won another Oscar nomination for his role in "Seven Days in May" (1964). He made 70 films, including a couple of shots as a director, over a cinema career of 40 years and was also a noted radio series star due to his voice which was ranked as one of the greatest in the movie/radio industry. His second wife Olga, a dancer and comedienne who appeared in two of her husband's films, bore him three children before a 1976 divorce ended their 28 year marriage.

Film Star Edmund O'Brien with his charming wife disembark for a holiday in Ireland.

Larry Parks

Larry Parks was Jolson and his impersonation of the minstrel stage legend won him a 1946 Academy Award nomination. Yet, despite a follow up triumph in "Jolson Sings Again" his screen career was in ruins in 1951 when he was the first actor to admit to Senator Joe McCarthy's Un-American Activities hearings that he had once had Communist Party affiliations. His studio contract was torn up and his name added to the unofficial blacklist that ostracised many major movie talents in the wake of the "Reds" witch-hunt. He turned to his wife, the singer-actress Betty Garrett who he had married in 1944, to form a stage partnership that initially toured the nightclubs and theatres of Europe before they would eventually return to Broadway where Parks had been cast in his first bit-part role back in 1937. Born into a family of German-Irish descent in Kansas but raised in Illinois, Samuel Klausman Lawrence Parks surmounted boyhood illness and would work on the fringes of the theatre world before getting his break. In Hollywood from 1941, roles were limited to costume adventures and second features before he got the role of Al Jolson. He was 60 when he died of a heart attack in 1975.

Gordon Scott

The fourth movie Tarzan, Gordon Scott, was the classic Hollywood discovery. The 6ft 3ins former army drill instructor had worked as a fireman, cowboy and farm machinery salesman before he was spotted by talent agents while working as a lifeguard in a Las Vegas

hotel. That was in 1953 when he was 27 years old and still Gordon Merrill Werschkul from Portland, Oregon. The producers of the Tarzan movies had already tested 200 candidates for the ape-man role when he was signed to take over from Lex Barker. Although he was given a 7 year contract, after five Tarzan screen adventures he turned down the chance to continue in the role and took off for the Europe where his physique made him a natural for "sword and sandal" epics loosely based on Greek and Roman myth. He also got star billing in spaghetti westerns and English language-dubbed espionage adventures in the James Bond vein. Besides making his first co-star, Vera Miles, his wife from 1954 to 1959, his first three Tarzan movies were rated mediocre even though the second was the first of the series to be shot in colour. But the last two were ranked among the best. He died aged 80 in 2007.

Ronald Colman

Personifying English gallantry and charm, Ronald Colman was a dashing swash-buckler and romantic leading man who was equally at home in light comedy and heavy dramatic roles. An established amateur actor from his teens, he turned to the stage as a career after suffering serious wounds at the Battle of Messines in Flanders in World War I. During a successful American tour he was lured to Hollywood where his superb speaking voice carried him from the silent movie era into the "talkies" where he was a leading man for more than 20 years. He won two 1930 nominations for best actor Academy Awards - "Bulldog Drummond" and "Condemned" - and would star in "Clive of India" and "The Prisoner of Zenda", played Sidney Carton in "A Tale of Two Cities" and starred in the classic "Lost Horizon". He was an Oscar nominee again for "Random Harvest" (1940) and finally took the 1947 Oscar for "A Double Life" playing a deranged actor whose private life becomes entangled with his role as "Othello". He was also a broadcasting star, teaming up with his actress wife Benita Hume to play the neighbours in the "Jack Benny Programme" which led to their own "Halls of Ivy" radio series which transferred to television in 1954-55.

John Laurie

John Laurie would be more than 50 years into a distinguished career as a stage and screen actor before he achieved television

immortality when contributing his portrayal of the fatalist –"we're all doomed" – Private Frazer to the unforgettable line-up of characters who made the long-running classic BBC "Dad's Army" comedy series an all-time favourite. He was 71 years old when he introduced the gloomy undertaker to television audiences in the opening 1968 season of a nine-year run that included a film adaptation of the misadventures of the Home Guard in wartime Britain. A distinctive as well as a distinguished actor, he was on the stage from 1921 and in movies from his 1930s cinema debut in the Sean O'Casey classic Irish drama "Juno and the Paycock" directed by Alfred Hitchcock. The mill worker's son from Dumfries in Scotland became a leading Shakespearean actor and acted in over 150 productions at Stratford on Avon and the Old Vic. Featured in character roles in over 100 films, his friend Laurence Olivier also cast him in all four of his Shakespeare screen productions – "As You Like It" (1936); "Henry V" ('44); "Hamlet" ('48) and "Richard III" ('55). He was 83 when he died in 1980.

Fred Astaire

Two cinematic eras converged when the film version of the Irish fantasy "Finian's Rainbow" was released in 1968. In the title role Fred Astaire had 35 years in movies behind him which had been marked 19 years earlier with a 1949 Special Oscar. The director was Francis Ford Coppola. Then on his third picture he was on his way to a place among the director greats for his "Godfather" trilogy and "Apocalypse Now" (1982). Born Frederick Austerlitz and dancing from age 7 with his sister Arlene; the re-named Fred Astaire made his 1933 breakthrough in "Flying Down To Rio". He was the uncontested dancing master in a succession of movie confections that were lean as the star himself on plot but visually voluptuous on dance numbers in the Busby Berkeley style. His celebrated partnership with Ginger Rogers brought out the crowds to ten films and the leading man also stepped out with dancing queens of their time Rita Hayworth;

Judy Garland; Cyd Charisse; Jane Powell and Leslie Caron. Retiring briefly in the mid 1940s, he returned to the screen in musicals and dramatic roles and was 75 years old when his performance in "The Towering Inferno" won him a 1974 Academy Award nomination.

Laurence Harvey

On-screen he mostly played unpalatable characters and following his death at age 45, the verdict from those who worked with the heavy drinker was that in real life he was much the same. Born into a Jewish family which emigrated from Lithuania to South Africa, after wartime service in the entertainment section of the South African army he headed to London's Royal Academy of Dramatic Art. He made his screen debut in 1948 but made no major impression in subsequent films until the "Room at the Top" landmark in British cinema when upper class English accents made way for colloquial speech patterns in the black and white realism of working class drama. His 1959 portrayal of social climber Joe Lampton won him Academy Award and BAFTA nominations. He carved out a special cinema trivia place for himself when co-starring with

actresses who won Oscars – Simone Signoret for "Room at the Top"; Elizabeth Taylor in "Butterfield 8" and Julie Christie in "Darling". He played the pivotal role of Colonel Travis in John Wayne's "The Alamo" epic, but is best remembered as the central character in the original version of "The Manchurian Candidate". He died in 1973.

Liberace & Kirk Douglas

What a combination! On the right the most virile of movie stars, Kirk Douglas with his second wife Anne (Buydens) snapped at Shannon with the high-camp piano playing Liberace. The only thing they had in common were the jaw-breaker names that were discarded when they built very different careers in the entertainment business. Kirk Douglas was born Issur Danielovitch in Amsterdam, New York, in 1916 and the pianist's parents of Polish and Italian extraction named him Wladziu Valentino Liberace when he was born three years later. The darling of matrons and blue-rinse generations on each side of the Atlantic, at the height of his 1950s fame Liberace commanded $50,000 a week in Las Vegas and brought his inimitable sequined and lacquered glamour to the first televised "Royal Command Performance" at the London Palladium in 1960. Kirk Douglas was a more frequent Fifties transatlantic traveller, coming to Europe to star in big budget epics "Ulysses", "The Vikings" and "Spartacus". Three-times nominated for an Academy Award he received a special Oscar in recognition of 50 years in films in 1996. Even though he suffered a stroke that year, he continued to appear in movies into the 21st century. Liberace died in 1986.